Mammal Mania

OTHER TITLES IN THE
YOUNG NATURALISTS SERIES

Amazing Amphibians: 30 Activities and Obeservations for
Exploring Frogs, Toads, Salamanders, and More

Awesome Snake Science! 40 Activities
for Learning About Snakes

Birdology: 30 Activities and Observations
for Exploring the World of Birds

Insectigations: 40 Hands-on Activities
to Explore the Insect World

Plantology: 30 Activities and Observations
for Exploring the World of Plants

Treecology: 30 Activities and Observations for
Exploring the World of Trees and Forests

Mammal Mania

30 Activities and Observations for Exploring the World of Mammals

Lisa J. Amstutz

CHICAGO
REVIEW
PRESS

Library of Congress Control Number: 2020952455

Cover design: Jonathan Hahn
Cover photos: FRONT: giraffe, Melanie van de Sande/Pixabay; squirrel,
Gilles Gonthier/Flickr; sloth, Stefan Laube (Tauchgurke)/Wikimedia
Commons; dolphins, Pexels/Pixabay. BACK: elephant, laurentmarx/
Pixabay; service dog, Found Animals Foundation/Flickr.
Interior design: Sarah Olson
Interior illustrations: Jim Spence

Printed in the United States of America
5 4 3 2 1

To those who will inherit
this marvelous Earth

Contents

Acknowledgments ix

Introduction xi

1: What Is a Mammal? 1
Try This! The Great Stuff Sort. 3

Try This! In Cold Blood 5

Try This! Make a Mammal-Watching Kit. 7

2: Meet the Mammals 9
Try This! Eat Like a Whale 11

Try This! Sending Sound Waves 13

Try This! Using a Dichotomous Key. 19

3: Parts of a Mammal 21
Look For: Take a Night Hike. 23

Listen For: Put on Your Deer Ears. 26

Try This! Build Like a Beaver 29

4: Home Sweet Home 31
Try This! Warm as a Whale. 35

Try This! Watch 'Em Sweat 36

Try This! Following the Clues. 38

5: Mammals Munch 41
Try This! Fridge Food Chain. 44

Try This! Become a Tooth Sleuth. 46

Try This! Find a Food Chain. 49

6: The Web of Life 51
Try This! Why Are Polar Bears White? 54

Try This! Write a Putrid Poem 55

Look For: Make a Tracking Station. 58

7: Life Goes On 61

Try This! Follow Your Nose 62

Look For: Be a Mammal Detective 64

Try This! A Day in the Life 69

8: Mammal Chat 71

Try This! Talk Like a Bat 73

Listen For: Make a Sound Map 76

Listen For: Underwater Sounds 77

9: Working with Mammals 79

Try This! Write to an Animal Scientist 80

Try This! Mammals in the News 84

Try This! Write a Mammal Song 85

10: How You Can Help 87

Try This! Research an Endangered Mammal 90

Try This! Make a Squirrel Feeder 91

Try This! Learn About Your State Mammal 95

Glossary 97

Orders of Mammals 99

Online Resources 101

Teacher's Guide 103

Bibliography 105

Index 107

Acknowledgments

I am so grateful for the love and support of my husband and kids, who continually inspire me. Huge thanks to my critique partners for their encouragement and thoughtful feedback, and to Dr. Lisa L. Walsh for sharing her scientific expertise. And finally, many thanks to Victoria Selvaggio for her ongoing support and friendship and to editor Jerome Pohlen, who brought this book to life.

A pair of dolphins surface. *Pexels/Pixabay*

Introduction

If you want to see a mammal up close and personal, take a look in the mirror! While we don't often think of ourselves as animals, humans are classified as mammals and have many things in common with other animals in this group. Of course, we have some important differences that set us apart, too.

Mammals live almost everywhere on Earth—from the icy waters of Antarctica to the scorching desert sands. They can be as small as a bumblebee or as big as an airplane. Some mammals, such as cats and dogs, make good pets. Others help humans do work. Horses and oxen can pull plows; dogs can help people with disabilities, herd sheep, or sniff out bombs.

These fascinating creatures are also important parts of **ecosystems** and food chains. Some eat plants, and others eat animals. Some **pollinate** plants. Many provide food for other animals, including humans. Hamburgers, yogurt, cheese, bacon, and ham all come from mammals—do you know which ones?

While mammals have been studied more closely than many groups, we still have much to learn about them. New high-tech tools are helping scientists study how mammals are related to each other and how they live—and even how their ancestors lived. These tools can also show us how to help mammals that are threatened by diseases, pollution, and **habitat** loss. Scientists and conservationists are working hard to find ways to protect endangered species before it is too late.

In this book, you'll find lots of fascinating facts about mammals. Each chapter includes three activities to help you discover more. It can be difficult to identify mammal species, and there are too many to include them all here. But you will learn how to study them carefully and observe their differences.

It's fun to go looking for mammals, but always tell an adult where you are going. You don't need to go far—you can probably find mammals or signs of mammals in your local park or even your backyard. Look for burrows or tunnels in the ground, and check trees for squirrels or other mammals that sleep or nest there. Morning and evening are good times to look for animals such as deer, rabbits, bats, and raccoons, which are active when the light is dim. Also look for tracks, pieces of fur, claw marks on trees, and scat (animal poop).

IMPORTANT! If you see a wild mammal, no matter how cute and cuddly it looks, **do not touch it.** Wild animals may bite if they are frightened or cornered. Some can carry disease as well. If you find an injured animal, ask an adult to help you contact your local wildlife rehabilitation center.

A herd of elephants in Kenya. *Rick Bergstrom/ Flickr*

1

What Is a Mammal?

Ch-ch-ch-ch-ch. A squirrel chatters in a tree. A robin gathers twigs to build its nest. A garter snake slithers by. All of these are animals, but only one of them is a mammal. Can you guess which one? If you guessed the squirrel, you are correct! A robin is a bird, and a garter snake is a reptile.

Mammals come in many shapes and sizes. Whales are mammals, and so are mice. These animals look very different. One is big and one is small. One lives in water and the other on land. One has no legs; the other has four. Yet despite their differences, they have some key things in common. In this chapter, you will explore what makes a mammal a mammal—and not a bird, fish, reptile, insect, or amphibian.

A sea lion is a marine mammal. *oliver.dodd/Flickr*

Squirrel. *Gilles Gonthier/Flickr*   **Robin.** *Kristof vt/Wikimedia Commons*   **Garter snake.** *Steve Jurvetson/Wikimedia Commons*

Linnaeus's Big Idea

For thousands of years, scientists did not have a good way to sort living things into groups. This made it hard to record and study them. People tried many different systems. Then, in the 1700s, a Swedish scientist named Carl Linnaeus came along. Linnaeus loved to study plants. He wanted to organize his plant collection. So, he came up with a plan. This turned into a whole new way of classifying all living things.

Linnaeus's big idea was to group things based on what they had in common. He first divided them into big groups called kingdoms. Linnaeus had three kingdoms: plants, animals, and stones. Today, most scientists use six kingdoms. These kingdoms only include living things, not rocks. Scientists have other ways to categorize those.

Each kingdom is divided into smaller and more specialized groups: kingdom, phylum, class, order, family, genus, and species. As the groups get smaller, their members become more and more alike. For instance, a class is a fairly large group within a kingdom. The mammals have their own class: Mammalia. They are different from birds, amphibians, reptiles, insects, or fish. But mammals can be very different from one another.

A weasel and a walrus are mammals that belong to the same order (Carnivora), which is named after the many meat-eating animals in the group. But they don't have much else in common! Lions and tigers, on the other hand, belong to the same order (Carnivora), family (Felidae), and genus (*Panthera*). Animals in the same genus are closely related. These big cats look and act in similar ways. Members of the same species—two snow leopards, for example—are as alike as two animals can be. They can breed with one another and make more animals of the same species.

Not everyone liked Linnaeus's ideas about grouping living things at first. They preferred their own ways of doing things. But as his students traveled the world and passed his ideas on, eventually the naming system caught on. And although some of the details have changed, we are still using Linnaeus's system today.

Linnaeus's Next Big Idea

After he got his plants sorted properly, Linnaeus decided to tackle their names, which were long and complicated in his day. The tomato, for instance, was called *Solanum caule inermi herbaceo, foliis pinnatis incises.* And people in different places called the same plants by different names. So Linnaeus decided every living thing should have two names: a genus and species. These names would be in Latin, a language that many scientists used at that time.

This way of naming things is called **binomial nomenclature**. The scientific name for the American robin is *Turdus migratorius.*

Your scientific name is *Homo sapiens.* And a house cat is *Felis catus.* These names usually describe the species in some way. *Turdus migratorius* means "migratory thrush"—most robins head south in the winter. *Homo* is Latin for "man," and *sapiens* means "wise." And you don't have to speak Latin to guess what *catus* means!

THE SIX KINGDOMS

Most scientists recognize six kingdoms today.

- **Archaebacteria:** Single-celled organisms that can live in some extreme environments
- **Eubacteria:** "True" bacteria—those found in the water, air, and soil around us
- **Protista:** Tiny plantlike or animallike organisms
- **Fungi:** Yeasts, molds, and mushrooms
- **Plantae:** Plants
- **Animalia:** Complex, multi-celled animals

TRY THIS!

The Great Stuff Sort

Carl Linnaeus came up with a great system for sorting plants and animals. Try to come up with a fun way to sort your stuff. Then see if a friend or family member can figure it out.

MATERIALS

- 20 random objects from around the house—for example: a toy car, egg beater, spoon, eraser, book, pack of chewing gum, or stuffed animal

1. Gather your pile of items.
2. Study the items. What do any of them have in common? Divide them into two groups. You might group them by color, size, material, or some other characteristic.
3. Now find a friend or family member. See if they can figure out what each group has in common.
4. Next, divide those groups into smaller ones. Continue until you have four or five groups. Ask your friend or family member to guess again.
5. Switch places and have your partner group the items in a different way. Then see if you can figure out their system.

The job of some scientists is to study how species should be grouped. They do this based on how organisms look and act. Today, they study organisms' genes to figure out how they are related. The science of naming and classifying living things is called **taxonomy**. Scientists who work in this field are called taxonomists**.**

To Be or Not to Be . . . a Mammal

Now, back to the first question: what makes an animal a mammal? All mammals have several things in common. They have a backbone and hair or fur. They also feed their babies milk and make their own body

HOW ARE *YOU* CLASSIFIED?

Kingdom: Animalia
Phylum: Chordata
Class: Mammalia
Order: Primates
Family: Hominidae
Genus: Homo
Species: sapiens

heat, as well as sharing some other hidden features. We'll take a closer look at each of these characteristics.

Show Some Backbone!

Your spine, or backbone, is a column of bones in the middle of your back. Each bone in the column is called a **vertebra**. These bones let you bend and twist in different directions. They also help you sit and stand upright. Imagine if you didn't have a backbone to hold you up. You'd have to lie flat all the time! And if you had no bones at all, you'd squish like a jellyfish.

Animals that have vertebrae are called vertebrates. All vertebrates are part of a large group, or phylum, called Chordata. Animals in this group include the birds, amphibians, reptiles, fish, and mammals.

If an animal does not have a backbone, it is not a mammal. But not all animals with backbones are mammals. So, more clues are needed to tell them apart.

Feel the Heat

What happens when you run around and get really hot? You probably start sweating. Your may turn red and you breathe hard. On a cold day, on the other hand, you might get goosebumps and shiver. You do

these things because, like all mammals, you are warm blooded.

Warm-blooded animals, called **endotherms**, make their own body heat by burning energy from food. *Endo* means "inside"—these animals make heat inside their bodies. They use behaviors such as shivering to help warm up when it is cold outside. They pant or sweat to cool down when they are too hot. These behaviors help keep their body the right temperature. Birds, mammals, and a few fish are endotherms.

You could think of warm-blooded animals as having their own furnace inside them, while cold-blooded animals must sit by the fire to warm up. Cold-blooded animals cannot make their own heat. Instead, they must move into the sun or hide in the shade to change their body temperature. If it is 100° F (38° C) in the sun, the temperature of a snake basking there will be 100° F. If it is 45° F (7° C) in a hole, the temperature of a snake resting there will be 45° F. Cold-blooded mammals are known as **ectotherms.** (*Ecto* means "outside"—they get heat from outside their bodies.) Insects and other invertebrates, amphibians, reptiles, and most fish are ectotherms.

There are some advantages to being warm blooded. Endotherms don't have to

In Cold Blood

Cold-blooded animals such as snakes cannot adjust their body temperature on their own. They must move to places where the air is cooler or warmer. On a cool day, they may bask in the sun. On a hot day, they may hide under a rock. Try this activity to see how the temperature affects a cold-blooded animal's body temperature.

MATERIALS

- 🖐 Modeling clay
- 🖐 Thermometer
- 🖐 Notebook
- 🖐 Pencil

1. Shape the modeling clay into three snakes.

2. Choose three places outdoors where a snake could rest. Place one in the sun, one in a shaded spot, and one in an in-between spot.

3. Let your snakes sit for a few hours. Then feel each one. Which feels coolest? Which feels warmest?

4. Set your thermometer on each snake. Record the temperature in your notebook. Which was highest?

The fur on an Arctic hare turns white in the winter to match the snow. *Steve Sayles/Flickr*

sit in the sun to warm up before they are able to move. They can be active at night, or in cold weather. And they can move much faster than ectotherms, in general. But sometimes they get too hot or too cold. And it takes a lot of energy—which comes from eating food—to heat and cool an endotherm's body.

Hide or Hair

Another feature of mammals is hair. Some have a lot of it, and some only a tiny bit. But they all have it somewhere, at some point in their lives. Cats are covered in fur, while whales have hardly any—just a few whiskers, which they lose soon after they are born.

Hair can help keep mammals warm, especially if they live in cold climates. It can also protect their skin from damage from the sun's rays. The hair on our heads may help with both of these. Some mammals, like dogs and cattle, grow thicker fur in the winter and shed some of it in the summer.

Another purpose for hair is camouflage. Arctic mammals such as the Arctic hare often grow white fur in winter to match the snow. They grow brown fur in summer to blend in with the soil and vegetation. Other mammals have fur that matches their habitat year-round.

SPECIES SPOTLIGHT: Three-Toed Sloth

The sloth is the world's slowest mammal. It is so slow moving that algae grow in its fur! The algae give its fur a greenish tinge. This color helps the sloth blend in with the trees. The algae also produce **nutrients**, which the sloth may eat or absorb through its skin. Certain species of moths live in the sloth's fur as well. These sloth moths produce organic material that feeds the algae. Teaming up in this way helps all three organisms to survive.

Sloths live in the rain forests of Central and South America. They spend 90 percent of their life hanging motionless in trees. Sloths even give birth while hanging from branches! For the first nine months of their life, the babies cling onto their mother as she moves around. The mother forms a sort of hammock for her baby by hanging upside-down.

It's almost always naptime if you're a sloth. Sloths sleep 15–20 hours per day. Even when awake, they don't move much. They graze on leaves, shoots, and fruits and get most of their water from these foods. They climb down to the ground about once a week, dig a hole, and go to the bathroom. They then cover the hole.

Sloths are well suited to the tree-dwelling life. Their long, curved claws make it easy to cling onto branches. Thanks to some extra vertebrae in their spine, they can turn their heads up to 270 degrees—that's three quarters of a circle. So a sloth can look around and see predators coming from almost any direction.

A three-toed sloth clings to a tree.
Stefan Laube (Tauchgurke)/Wikimedia Commons

Got Milk?

Another feature that all mammals share is that the females feed their babies milk. They make the milk in mammary glands. (This is where the word "mammal" comes from!) This milk is packed with nutrients such as calcium, protein, iodine, potassium, phosphorus, and vitamins B2 and B12. The young mammal needs these nutrients to grow. When the baby is old enough, it will eat other foods as well. This process of shifting to solid food is called weaning. Humans are the only mammals that continue to drink milk after they're weaned. And we are the only mammals that regularly drink the milk of another animal species.

Because they need their mother's milk to survive, baby mammals must stay near their mother. Their mother (and sometimes father) feeds them, protects them from danger, and teaches them the skills they need to survive. For this reason, young mammals stay with their parents much longer than many other animals, such as fish or frogs.

Hidden Features

Two other things set mammals apart from other classes of animals, but they can't be seen on the outside. Mammals have a dome-shaped structure in their abdomen

WATCHING WILD ANIMALS

Wild mammals are interesting and fun to watch. But it's important not to get too close. These animals can bite or kick if they feel threatened. They will also fiercely protect their young, so never get between a mother and her babies. Use binoculars to watch from a safe distance.

Some mammals make good pets. But keeping wild animals as pets is dangerous and may even be illegal. When you meet someone else's pet, be sure to check with the owner to make sure it's friendly. Then, approach it slowly and carefully.

called a diaphragm. This sheet of muscles separates their chest from their digestive organs. When the diaphragm contracts, the chest cavity gets larger and the lungs suck in air. When it relaxes, air is pushed out of the lungs. The diaphragm is also involved in coughing, sneezing, crying, vomiting, hiccupping, and pushing out urine and feces.

The second hidden feature of mammals is some specialized bones, including three

Make a Mammal-Watching Kit

You can watch mammals anywhere—at the zoo, at a park or nature center, at a pet store—even in your backyard. Some zoos and parks have webcams too. You can learn a lot by watching animals. Keep track of what you see. Then you can compare the behavior of animals at different places and times.

MATERIALS

- Blank notebook
- Pencil or pen
- Colored pencils, markers, or crayons
- Field guide
- Binoculars (optional)
- Camera (optional)

1. Choose a place to watch for mammals. Sit very still and be quiet so you don't startle them.

2. When you spot a mammal, make notes about its behavior and appearance. Does it hop, jump, or scurry? How big is it? What color is its fur? Where do you think it lives?

3. Sketch a picture of the mammal in your notebook. Be sure to write down where and when you saw it.

4. Color in your picture with colored pencils, markers, or crayons.

5. Use a field guide to identify the animal if it is unfamiliar. You may want to take a picture of it to add to your notebook.

tiny bones in the middle ear, just behind the eardrum. These bones carry sound vibrations from the eardrum to the inner ear, where they are picked up by another bone called the cochlea. Their two extra ear bones allow mammals to hear softer sounds than reptiles or birds can.

2

Meet the Mammals

Mammals come in all shapes and sizes. They range from tiny bats and shrews to enormous elephants and whales. The smallest are as light as a penny; the largest weigh as much as a house! There are more than 6,000 different species of mammals worldwide, belonging to 27 different orders. Nearly 700 species live in North America. There's not enough space in this book to talk about all of the world's mammals, but in this chapter you'll take a look at some of the major groups.

Two antelope lock horns at a game reserve in Botswana. *David Minty/Flickr*

Plenty of Placentals

Most mammals are what scientists call **placentals**. These animals develop inside their mothers' bodies and are nourished through a special organ called a placenta. This organ is filled with blood vessels that carry nutrients. It is joined to the baby by an umbilical cord. Take a look at your belly button—that's where your umbilical cord was attached.

Notorious Nibblers

Nibble, nibble, squeak! Have you ever had a mouse in the house? Then you've met a

The prairie dog belongs to the rodent family.
mordilla-net/Pixabay

rodent. The rodents (Order Rodentia) are the largest group of placental mammals. This pint-sized group includes squirrels, mice, rats, beavers, porcupines, gophers, and many others: more than 2,500 species in all.

Guinea pigs, hamsters, and gerbils make popular pets. Other rodents, such as mice and rats, can be pets *or* pests. The beaver is much larger and can cut down trees to build lodges and dams. The largest rodent of all is the capybara, which lives in South America and can weigh as much as 110 pounds (50 kg). Capybaras look like giant guinea pigs, which isn't surprising when you learn that they belong to the same family.

All of these rodent relatives have one thing in common: a pair of big buck teeth that never stop growing. That's a good

PREHISTORIC MAMMALS

Mammals have been around for a long time. Small shrew-like animals called morganucodontids were the earliest known mammals. They lived when dinosaurs roamed the Earth. After the large dinosaurs died off, mammals grew much larger and more dominant. Like other prehistoric animals, some of them were huge compared to today's versions. A relative of the rhinoceros, the Indricotherium, was about four times the weight of a modern elephant, with a long neck and a horse-like head. It was 26 feet (8 m) long and 18 feet (5.5 m) high at the shoulder. Meanwhile, the Glyptodon, a prehistoric armadillo, was the size of a small car!

The glyptodon was a giant prehistoric relative of the armadillo.
WolfmanSF/Wikimedia Commons

thing, since rodents feed mainly on seeds and plants, which wear down the ends of their teeth. If their teeth didn't keep growing, rodents would soon be toothless. As it is, they must nibble almost continually so their teeth don't get too long.

Night Flyers

It's a bird. . . . It's a plane. . . . No, it's a bat! Bats swoop and glide through the air in search of food. Order Chiroptera—the bats—has almost 1,400 members. That makes it the second-largest group of mammals. The name Chiroptera means "hand wing." That's because the bones inside a bat's wings are very similar to those in your hands.

Wait—wings? That's right! Bats are the only mammals that can truly fly (although a few others, like flying squirrels, can glide for long distances). Unlike birds, bats do not have feathers. Their bodies are furry, and their wings are covered with two layers of leathery skin. Just as you can twist and move your hands and fingers in many different ways, bats can change their wing shape while they fly in order to catch even the slightest breeze. This makes them very efficient flyers. Some fly hundreds of miles when they **migrate**.

 TRY THIS!

Eat Like a Whale

There are two types of whales. Baleen whales eat by straining tiny animals from the water with their fringed teeth. Toothed whales use large, sharp teeth to bite into their prey. Try this activity to see how each method works.

MATERIALS

- Bucket
- Dried oregano
- Small objects such as packing peanuts, beads, pennies, or small toys
- Comb
- Pasta strainer
- Tongs

1. Fill the bucket with water.
2. Sprinkle in the small objects and oregano.
3. Try picking up objects and herbs using the comb, pasta strainer, and tongs.
4. Which tool worked best for capturing each object?

The largest bats, called megabats, are the size of a squirrel. The smallest microbats are the size of a bumblebee. Most bats are nocturnal—they hunt at night and sleep during the day, often in large groups. Some eat the leaves, nectar, fruit, or pollen of plants, while others eat smaller mammals, insects, fish—and even other bats! They find their food by sending out squeaks and clicks and listening to the echoes that bounce off insects and other objects. The bat's brain uses these echoes to form a "sound picture" of where objects are located and whether they are moving or still. This is called echolocation.

A few species of bats feed on the blood of larger animals by making a small cut and lapping up the blood that flows out.

These vampire bats are named after the mythical monsters that come out at night to feed on human blood.

Many people are afraid of bats, but they are an important part of the ecosystem. They pollinate crops such as bananas, mangoes, and guava. Without bats, these crops could not grow. Bats are also good for pest control. Some eat half their weight in insects every night. That's a lot of mosquitoes! How much do you weigh? Divide that number in half. Could you chow down that much hamburger every day?

A Whale of a Family

Not all mammals live on land. Some live in rivers and oceans. The cetaceans—the whales, dolphins, and porpoises—include both toothed whales and baleen whales. As their name suggests, toothed whales have teeth. Dolphins, porpoises, sperm whales, and orcas belong to this group. Baleen whales filter food from the water using large, fringed plates called baleen. They plow through shoals of fish, plankton, and krill, filling their mouths and then pushing out the water with their tongue. Their prey is trapped inside the filter. Interestingly, the very largest whales are filter feeders.

They may look "fishy," but like all mammals, cetaceans feed their babies milk. Their front limbs are shaped like flippers, but inside, the bones look similar to those of your hand. They breathe through a blowhole in the top of their head. That means they must come to the surface for air. Dolphins can only stay underwater for about 15 minutes, while some whales can hold their breaths for two hours or more.

Cattle of the Sea

Another group of sea mammals is the Sirenians—the manatees and dugongs. These animals are also known as "sea cows," because they are large animals that graze like cows. Although it's hard to see the resemblance, ancient Greek sailors sometimes mistook these huge, slow-moving animals for mermaids. Manatees feed on underwater plants and come to the surface every few minutes for air. Dugongs look and act similarly, but their tails have a different shape. Manatees can be found along the east coast of the Americas from Florida to Brazil, in the Amazon River, and along the west coast of Africa. Dugongs live from the coast of East Africa to Australia.

A humpback whale leaps out of the water. Whales are marine mammals. *skeeze/Pixabay*

TRY THIS!

Sending Sound Waves

*Sound waves are waves of energy that travel through a material such as air or water. A wave pushes the molecules ahead of it out of place for an instant before they spring back. Those molecules push the ones ahead of them, so the wave moves through the **medium** like a row of dominoes falling. When sound waves hit your eardrums, tiny bones and nerves turn them into electrical signals that your brain interprets as sound. Try this activity with a friend to see how sound waves work.*

MATERIALS
- Slinky

1. Have each person take one end of the Slinky and gently stretch it out. There should be about 1 inch (2.5 cm) between the coils.

2. Start a wave on one end by pulling a coil back with your finger and letting it go.

3. Watch as the wave travels through the Slinky to the other end.

Lions, Tigers, and Bears . . . Oh My!

The word **carnivore** means "meat eater," and many species in Order Carnivora are specialized meat eaters. The feliform, or catlike, carnivores include animals such as lions, tigers, cheetahs, mongooses, hyenas, and civets. House cats fit into this group as well. These animals have sharp teeth and claws that help them catch and kill their prey. They can pull their claws back into their paws when they aren't needed, which helps them sneak up quietly on prey animals.

On the other hand, doglike, or caniform, carnivores have a longer snout and cannot retract their claws. This group includes dogs, bears, wolves, foxes, weasels, badgers, and raccoons.

Surprisingly, this order also includes the seals, sea lions, and walruses. These animals have both front and rear flippers. Although they live in the ocean, they also spend a lot of time on land. Seals, sea lions, and walruses feed on krill, fish, and even penguins. In turn, they are eaten by many larger animals such as killer whales, sharks, and polar bears.

Hoofed Herbivores

Do you know how many toes a deer has? How about a zebra? Large, hoofed **herbivores** (plant eaters) can be divided into two groups based on their number of toes: the even-toed and odd-toed hoofed mammals.

The even-toed hoofed mammals have either two or four toes on each foot. The toes are covered with a hornlike substance that protects them. The even-toed hoofed mammals include deer, cows, goats, bison, sheep, camels, llamas, pigs, and hippopotamuses. There are about 500 different terrestrial species in this group (Order Artiodactyla).

The odd-toed hoofed mammals (Order Perissodactyla) are a smaller group of about 20 species. These animals have either one or three toes on their hind feet. They include zebras, horses, tapirs, and rhinoceroses.

13

Like their even-toed cousins, these animals munch on grasses, leaves, and branches. A special pouch in their gut holds bacteria that help them digest tough plant material.

Monkey Business

Now it's time to get personal. About 500 species of mammals fit into Order Primates—the lemurs, lorises, tarsiers, apes, and monkeys. Scientists put humans in this group as well. We primates all have large brains, and many of us can use tools. We can wrap our fingers around objects, like a glass or baseball bat. That's thanks to our **opposable** thumbs, which can bend across our fingers. Primates are also some of the only mammals with fingernails—few other animals could get a manicure!

Monkeys are divided into two groups: New World and Old World. The New World monkeys live in Central and South America. They have flatter noses and long tails that are often **prehensile**. These tails can grasp branches as the animal swings through the trees. The Old World monkeys live in Africa and Asia. They have narrow noses, and their tails are never prehensile.

Apes are typically larger in size than monkeys, and most are good at climbing trees. They have strong arms and chests that let them easily hang or swing from branch to branch. Apes do not have tails, while almost all monkeys do. Chimpanzees, orangutans, gorillas, and gibbons are all apes. Humans are classified as apes too.

And Many More . . .

There are many more kinds of mammals—too many to name here. Some of the smaller orders of mammals include only a few species. The aardvark, for instance, is the only living member of its order (Tubulidentata). It lives in parts of Africa, where it rips open ant and termite nests and slurps them up with its long, sticky tongue.

Pangolins (Order Pholidota) look similar to armadillos—and artichokes!—but they are in a group all their own. Pangolins live in Africa and Asia. When threatened, they curl up in a ball and squirt smelly fluid from a gland near their anus. The stink helps keep predators away.

There are two species of colugos (Order Dermoptera), big-eyed little mammals that live in the jungles of Southeast Asia. They spread out their legs and glide from tree to tree. Colugos can travel up to two-thirds the length of a football field in a single swoop!

The elephants (Order Proboscidea) are named after their huge nose (proboscis).

They also have large ears and two big tusks. Elephants live in Asia and Africa. They feed on grasses, bushes, and trees. There are only two or three species of elephants, depending on whom you ask. The African elephant is slightly larger and has much bigger ears than its Asian cousin. Both male and female African elephants have tusks, while only male Asian ones do.

Another group of long-nosed animals is the elephant shrews, which actually are related to elephants. You won't get the two mixed up, though—the largest elephant shrew weighs only 1.5 pounds (0.7 kg)—about the same as a basketball! Elephant shrews feed on insects and earthworms.

Marvelous Marsupials

While placental mammals grow inside their mother until they are ready to be born, marsupials have a different strategy. Most (but not all) female marsupials have a pouch. No, they don't keep their keys or wallet in it—it's a warm and cozy baby carrier! Marsupial babies are born before they are fully developed. They are blind, hairless, and unable to survive out in the world. So they live in their mother's marsupium, or pouch, which is a flap of skin that covers the mother's teats to form a pocket for .

SPECIES SPOTLIGHT: Tasmanian Devil

Cartoons often show the Tasmanian devil as a whirling, snarling beast. There's a reason for that: Tasmanian devils whip themselves into a ferocious frenzy when they're attacked by a predator, guarding their food, or fighting for a mate. European settlers dubbed them "devils" after seeing this behavior. Tasmanian devils often yawn at predators, showing their wide mouths and sharp teeth. You don't want to mess with a Tasmanian devil—for its size, it has the world's most powerful bite! However, it is unlikely to attack you unless you bother it.

Tasmanian devils live only on the Australian island of Tasmania, although they were once found on the mainland as well. They grow to about 26 pounds (12 kg) and look like baby bears. Devils feed on small mammals, birds, reptiles, amphibians, and insects.

They also eat meat from dead animals, called **carrion**. They have strong jaws and teeth and can even chew up the fur and bones of their prey. Devils hunt at night, traveling up to 10 miles (16 km) to find food.

Tasmanian devils are marsupials, and a female devil gives birth to up to 50 raisin-sized babies, called joeys or imps, at a time. But since she has only four teats, only the four strongest, fastest babies will survive. She carries them in her pouch for four months, and then hides them in a hollow log for another month or two until they are weaned.

Tasmanian devils are now an endangered species and protected by the Australian government. They are threatened not only by loss of habitat and lack of food, but also by a type of cancer. This disease is passed along when they bite each other.

A Tasmanian devil shows its teeth.
CraigRJD/iStock

15

A young wallaby pops its head out of its mother's pouch. Wallabies are marsupials.
sandid/Pixabay

enough, it may climb out and ride around on its mother's back between meals.

Marsupials are a varied bunch, with little in common besides their pouch. Kangaroos are probably the best known. But this group also includes opossums, Tasmanian devils, gliders, and bandicoots, to name a few. Marsupial brains are on the small side, and these animals don't tend to make much noise. Marsupials don't usually live in groups, although kangaroos and wallabies will hang out in loosely connected groups called mobs.

More than 350 species belong to this group of mammals, and over 200 of those live in or near Australia. In fact, most of the mammals native to Australia, New Guinea, and the nearby islands are marsupials. Only one marsupial—the Virginia opossum—lives in the United States and Canada.

The largest marsupial is the red kangaroo, which can grow as tall as an adult man

her young. These teats supply the mother's milk. The babies, called joeys, crawl or squirm to one of their mother's teats and latch on. Sometimes there are more babies than teats, so the race to latch on is literally a matter of life or death. Only the strongest survive.

Once the joey is latched on, the teat swells up so much that the joey can't let go, even if it wants to. It stays there for weeks or months, growing and developing until it is ready to face the world. Once it is big

AUSTRALIA: HOME OF THE WORLD'S WEIRDEST MAMMALS

Australia is home to some of the most unique animals in the world, from furry platypuses with the bill of a duck and fierce Tasmanian devils to hopping kangaroos and tree-dwelling koalas. Why did so many unusual animals end up here?

The short answer is: no one knows for sure. Scientists do not believe marsupials started off in Australia. Instead, they moved from North America to South America.

At that time, the Earth's continents formed one large land mass. So the marsupials moved through Antarctica (which was rather tropical at that time) to reach Australia.

The koala is a marsupial that lives in Australia.
Tambako The Jaguar/Flickr

and weighs around 200 pounds (90 kg). The smallest is the long-tailed planigale, which could fit in your hand. Other species fall somewhere in between.

The Extreme Monotremes

There is an exception to almost every rule, and monotremes are the rule-breakers of the mammal world. They are the only group of mammals that lays eggs. They also have no teats—milk simply oozes out of pores on the mother's belly and her babies lap it up.

While scientists believe the monotremes are the most ancient group of mammals, this group contains just two families today: the echidnas (spiny anteaters) and the platypuses. Both families are found only in Australia, Tasmania, and the island of New Guinea.

Monotreme Mash-Up

Imagine that you took a beaver and a duck and mixed them together—you might come out with something like a platypus. In fact, when European scientists first saw a platypus specimen, they thought it had to be a fake! But they were eventually convinced that this odd-looking mammal was real.

A platypus feeds on a worm. This unusual mammal is a monotreme. *JohnCarnemolla/iStock*

The platypus is a strong swimmer and has folds of skin that seal off its eyes, nose, and ears while underwater. It hunts for insects, worms, shellfish, and other small animals at the bottom of riverbeds. The platypus sifts through the mud with its leathery beak, finding food using special sensors in its bill. These help it sense electric currents put out by its prey. The animal stuffs the food in its cheeks, along with gravel from the river bed. The rocks mash the meal before it is swallowed.

The platypus has another interesting feature. Unlike most other mammals, it is **venomous**. A spur on a male's hind legs can inject poison into an attacker's skin.

The platypus has sharp nails on its webbed toes, which it uses to dig burrows in the river bank. Deep inside, the female lays one or two eggs. In about ten days, her lima bean–sized babies hatch out. She nurses them for three to four months until they are big enough to hunt on their own.

Extraordinary Echidnas

The echidna, or spiny anteater, is named after a monster from Greek mythology who was half woman and half serpent. But although its spines may be scary-looking, the echidna is quite shy. It hunts for ants and termites, tearing into rotten logs and ant mounds with its short legs and then slurping up its meal with its sticky tongue. The echidna doesn't have any teeth to chew its prey with, so it uses hard pads on its tongue and the roof of its mouth to mash them up.

An echidna's body is covered with hollow spines. These help protect the animal from predators. When threatened, it quickly digs a hole, leaving only its spiny rear end sticking out. No predator wants a mouthful of that!

Once a year, the female echidna lays a grape-sized egg, which she rolls into the

pouch on her belly. Ten days later, the baby (called a puggle) hatches out. The puggle holds onto its mother's hairs and laps milk produced by glands in her pouch. Fortunately for Mom, young puggles do not have spines. Once the spines start growing, the mother moves her prickly offspring to a burrow. She returns to feed it every five to ten days until it is about seven months old.

The echidna, or spiny anteater, is a monotreme. *Cazz/Flickr*

18

Using a Dichotomous Key

A dichotomous key is a tool that scientists use to identify animals. It works by sorting organisms into smaller and smaller groups based on things they have in common. At each step, two choices are given. The user chooses which one fits best and then follows that path. Try making your own key, then test it out on a friend.

MATERIALS

- Magazines with plant and animal pictures
- Scissors
- Paper
- Pen

1. Cut out 20 different plant and animal pictures from your magazines.

2. Sort the pictures into groups. How are they similar or different?

3. On your piece of paper, draw a dichotomous key to fit your categories.

4. Mix up your pictures. Then see if a friend can follow your key and sort them into the same categories you chose.

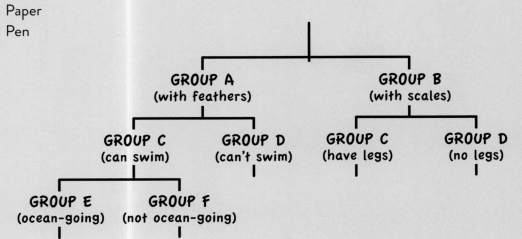

3

Parts of a Mammal

Now that you've met many different kinds of mammals, it's time to zoom in for a closer look. Like all animals, mammals have special **adaptations** that help them find food and mates and avoid being eaten. These adaptations help them survive in their environment.

The Eyes Have It

If you live underground like a mole does, you don't have much use for eyes. But above ground, they come in pretty handy. While moles can't see much, most mammals have good eyesight, though not as sharp as that of a hawk or eagle. The shape of a mammal's pupils (the hole that lets light

Male mandrills have brightly colored faces. *Mhy/Pixabay*

meineresterampe/Pixabay

Steve Gatto/Flickr

Tambako The Jaguar/Flickr

The pupil of a mammal's eye has a different shape depending on how it hunts. (Left to right: goat, cat, lemur)

in) and the direction its eyes point depend on what it eats—and its risk of being eaten by predators.

When you're a grazer, you must be alert to danger, even while your head is down in the grass. So antelope and other grazers have horizontal pupils that give them a wide field of vision. Because their eyes are on the sides of their heads, the picture they see is like a panoramic photo.

A house cat, on the other hand, has eyes on the front of its head. It has vertical pupils. This shape helps small mammals judge distance as they prepare to pounce on their prey. Larger predators whose eyes are farther from the ground, like tigers, have round pupils.

The tarsier, a small primate that lives in South Asia, has huge eyes for its size. It cannot swivel them, so it must turn its head to see side to side. It can turn its head so far it can almost see directly behind it! These large eyes are useful for hunting at night, when the tarsier is active. They take in lots of light.

Like the tarsier, most nocturnal animals have larger eyes and wider pupils than animals that are active during the day. They also have a sort of "mirror" behind their retina (the tissue at the back of their eye). This reflective layer is called a tapetum. As the light bounces back, it gives the eye a second chance to absorb it. This gives the animal good night vision. Have you ever seen an animal's eyes glowing at night when light hits them? That is because of the tapetum. A cat's eyes glow green, an

opossum's glow orange, and a raccoon's glow yellow. This glow is called eyeshine.

Mammal Mouths

Each mammal's teeth are specially adapted to its diet. They come in many different shapes and sizes—a trait unique to mammals. Flat, square teeth are good for nipping off grass or twigs. Sharp, pointy teeth can puncture the neck of a prey animal and kill it in an instant.

Some mammals have enormous teeth called tusks. These stick out of the animal's mouth even when its lips are closed. Elephant tusks can reach nearly 10 feet (3 m) in length. Elephants use these massive teeth not only for fighting but also to dig for food and mark their **territory** by slashing trees. The tusks are made of a material called ivory, which was used in the past to make carvings, piano keys, handles, and more. Elephants have become endangered partly because of people killing them for their tusks and partly because of habitat loss.

The narwhal, sometimes called the "unicorn whale," is also known for its long tusk, which can grow to 10 feet (3 m). Spiral grooves wrap around it, and sensitive nerve endings help it sense changes in water temperature, pressure, and chemistry.

Scientists aren't sure how narwhals use this information, but it may help them find food or mates. Or it might help them find breathing holes in the Arctic by steering clear of colder, saltier water.

Baleen whales do not have teeth at all—at least, not what we think of as teeth. They have a big, hard, comb-like structure called baleen. The baleen is made of **keratin**, just like your fingernails. It acts as a filter to strain tiny plants and animals out of the water for the whale to eat.

Terrific Tongues

A few mammals don't have teeth *or* baleen—there's no point when you swallow your food whole! Instead, these animals use their tongues to snag their next meal. Some bats, for instance, reach their tongues into flowers to sip nectar. And anteaters stick their two-foot-long sticky tongues into ant or termite mounds to catch their dinner.

How many times can you flick out your tongue in a minute? Is it as many as an anteater? The giant anteater can eat more than 35,000 ants or termites in a single day, flicking its tongue out 150 times per minute. Its tongue is 2 feet (60 cm) long.

Cats have an interesting feature on their tongues—hooks! When the cat runs its

LOOK FOR

Take a Night Hike

Have you ever taken a hike at night? It is a good time to see animals that you don't normally see. Be sure to take an adult along. If you're in a park or nature center, stay on the trail so you don't get lost.

MATERIALS
- Flashlight or headlamp
- Good walking shoes

1. With an adult's permission, take a walk after dark in a safe location.

2. Stand still and sweep the area with the beam of your flashlight. Look for glowing eyes. Note their color. When you get home, do some research to find out what animals they might belong to. Don't forget to look in the grass around you. The eyes of some spiders and insects glow too.

3. Do you see any white flowers blooming? These are usually pollinated by bats or moths. They are easy to see at night.

3. Shut off your flashlight and look up. Watch for bats or night-flying birds such as owls and nighthawks.

4. Now stand quietly and listen. What sounds do you hear? Can you identify where they are coming from?

23

tongue over its fur, these tiny barbed hooks grab and straighten the hairs like a brush. They also catch any loose hairs and remove them. The cat swallows them and will later cough up a "hairball." These hooks make a cat's tongue feel rough when it licks your hand.

A giraffe's black tongue is covered with a layer of extremely tough skin. Giraffes use their long tongues to pluck leaves from thorny acacia trees. This thick outer layer protects their tongue from damage.

Noteworthy Noses

Sniff, sniff, POUNCE! A polar bear's nose can sniff out a seal on the ice 20 miles (32 km) away or find a seal's air hole from up to 1 mile (1.6 km) away. Bears are thought to have the world's best sense of smell.

A close contender is the elephant, whose nose is, well, notable. An elephant can smell water 12 miles (19 km) away. Its trunk comes in handy for picking up food, touching other elephants, picking up water to squirt in its mouth or over its back, and trumpeting loudly.

All mammals breathe air through lungs—even those that live underwater. Unlike fish, which use gills to remove

WHAT IS AN OPPOSABLE THUMB?

Can you twiddle your thumbs? With a little practice, most people can. But how about your toes? Probably not! You can twiddle your thumbs because they are opposable—that is, you can move them separately from the rest of your fingers.

Opposable thumbs come in handy in many ways. Imagine trying to write, eat, or play basketball without them. It would be like doing these activities with your toes. To test this out, try taping your thumb to your palm for a while as you go about your daily activities. You will soon see how useful it is!

oxygen from the water, marine mammals must surface to breathe air. However, most marine mammals can hold their breath a lot longer than you can. Not only are their lungs much larger, but their blood carries more oxygen. When diving, the blood only takes oxygen to the essential parts—the heart, brain, and muscles used for swimming. In this way, whales can stay underwater for up to several hours. The sperm whale, for example, can hold its breath and dive up to 9,840 feet (3 km) to hunt giant squid.

Seals, sea lions, and walruses also have lungs, but instead of breathing through a blowhole, they simply raise their heads above water. Harbor seals sleep by floating at the surface with their heads above water so they can breathe. This is known as bottling.

Can You Hear Me Now?

Mammals have three middle ear bones, while other vertebrates have only one. Sound enters the outer ear, which funnels it to the middle ear. It hits the eardrum and transfers to the three small bones. In the inner ear, the soundwaves are transferred to nerves and then to the brain.

Mammals have good hearing compared to many other animals. Some, such as bats and dolphins, can hear sounds so high that humans cannot hear them (ultrasonic

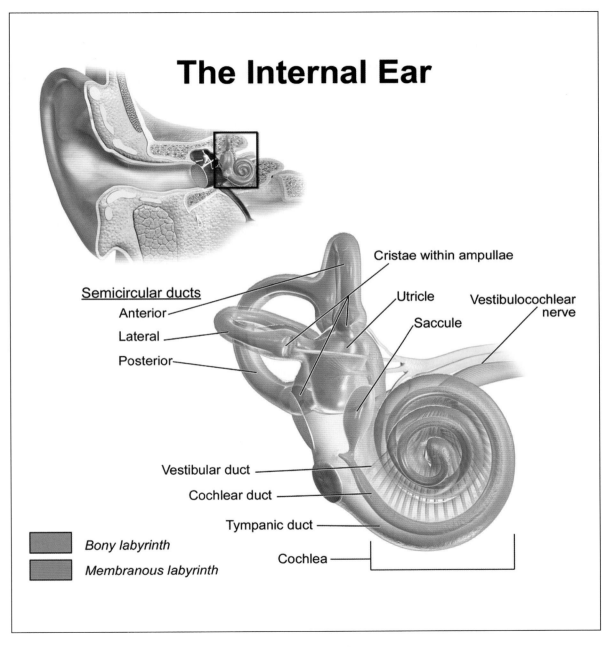

The Internal Ear

Semicircular ducts
- Anterior
- Lateral
- Posterior

Cristae within ampullae

Utricle

Saccule

Vestibulocochlear nerve

Vestibular duct

Cochlear duct

Tympanic duct

Cochlea

Bony labyrinth

Membranous labyrinth

Diagram of a human inner ear. *Blausen.com staff/Wikimedia Commons*

sounds). Mole rats, elephants, and baleen whales can hear lower sounds than humans can (infrasonic).

Sound travels well in water, but mammals that live in water have slightly different ear structures than those that live on land. Because of this, many of these mammals, such as whales, cannot hear well on land. Polar bears and walruses, which live on land and in the water, can hear well in either place.

Not a Hair Out of Place

Some mammals, like bears and tigers, are covered in thick, dense fur. But only a few whiskery hairs can be found on others, such as whales, elephants, and rhinos. Either way, all mammals have hair—at least some form of it, at some point in their lives.

Hair is a material made of keratin and other proteins. It grows from tiny pits in the skin called follicles. The live cells at the bottom of the hair keep dividing and growing new hair. As they die, they are pushed up.

Mammal hair comes in many lengths, shapes, and colors. While a pygmy shrew's fur may be only a fraction of an inch long, the musk ox's long locks can reach more than three feet (one meter) in length, nearly touching the ground. Hairs can be curly or

Put on Your Deer Ears

Deer have large ears that they can turn in almost any direction to follow sound. As prey animals, they must constantly be on the lookout for predators. Their large ears capture lots of sound. Try out some "deer ears" of your own to see how well they work!

MATERIALS

✋ Two hands

1. Cup one hand behind each ear. Listen to the sounds around you. Can you hear more sounds with your "deer ears"?

2. Now cup your hands the other way, so your palms are pointing backward. This is like a deer listening to sounds behind it. Can you hear sounds from behind you better now?

3. Try this activity indoors and outdoors. Do you notice any difference?

The heavy fur of a musk ox keeps it toasty warm in winter. *Jonas Rönnbro/iStock*

straight depending on the shape of the follicle that they grow out of. They can be soft or stiff.

Who Needs Hair?

Every feature of an animal's body has a purpose, and hair is no exception. Hair can help keep an animal warm. This is important because mammals are warm blooded and must make their own heat. For those that live in polar regions, warm fur can make the difference between life and death. A sea otter has up to a million hairs per square inch of skin! These tightly packed hairs keep icy water out.

We think of some animals as having fur and others as having hair. What's the difference? Technically, nothing. It's all made from keratin. But we tend to call short, thickly packed hairs "fur" and longer strands "hair." A "true fur" has an outer layer of guard hairs to shed water and a short, dense undercoat for warmth and insulation. A very thick coat of soft, curly fur may be called "wool," especially on a sheep.

Along with keeping them warm, fur can also help to camouflage mammals. Animals that live close to or under the ground are often brown or gray; their color makes them harder for predators to spot. Some change colors throughout the year to match their surroundings. The short-tailed weasel, for example, grows white fur in winter to match

ANIMAL BEAUTY SALONS

It takes a lot of care to keep a mammal's hair in good condition. Just like you wash and brush your hair, animals also groom themselves. They "comb" their fur with their tongues, rub oil from special glands over their fur, and remove parasites. An animal's coat is a good sign of how healthy it is—an animal with dirty, matted fur is likely old or sickly.

Some mammals also groom each other. At these "beauty salons," animals help each other reach those spots they can't quite reach on their own. Parents lick and groom their young. Grooming spreads the group's scent around so family members can recognize each other.

Many mammals like to take dust baths to clean their fur. They roll around in the dust and then shake it off to help remove dirt and parasites. What do you think—would you enjoy a dust bath?

the snow in its cold winter habitat, and brown fur in the summer to match the soil.

Some mammals have special types of hairs called whiskers that help the animal sense its surroundings. These stiff hairs feel breezes, sense nearby objects, and even feel the movement of other animals. The walrus uses its whiskery mustache to find prey on the ocean floor. A cat uses them to measure the size of an opening—can it fit through that door?

Mammals that don't have much or any hair usually have a tough layer of skin. The Sumatran rhinoceros has patches of short, stiff hairs on its thick hide. These hairs help mud stick to it when it takes a mud bath. The mud helps protect its skin from the sun and insects. It also cools the animal.

The Tail End

Did you ever fall on your "tailbone"? Humans don't have tails, but we do have several bones at the base of our spine known as the coccyx, usually called a tailbone. A mammal's tail is part of its spine and is made up of vertebrae.

The record for the longest tail on a land mammal belongs to the giraffe, at up to eight feet. But the long-eared jerboa is a contender too, with a tail that is twice as long as its mouse-sized body!

Tails can be useful tools. Horses' tails have brushy hair that is good for swishing away flies. Foxes use their bushy tails as nose- and toe-warmers on chilly days. A flying squirrel's long, furry tail acts as a

Short, stiff hairs on a rhino's hide help mud stick to it. *christels/Pixabay*

rudder and brake when it glides through the sky. A spider monkey uses its tail as an extra arm to hang from trees. A whale's powerful tail helps it swim. And elephants walk in single file by curling their trunk around the tail of the elephant in front.

Tails are also used to communicate with other animals. A dog may wag its tail when it is happy, while a beaver slaps its tail on the water to warn others of danger. Ring-tailed lemurs use scent glands on their tails to mark their territory.

SPECIES SPOTLIGHT: Vampire Bat

Blood-sucking vampires aren't real—are they? No, but the legends might have been based on the vampire bat. Vampire bats feed on animal blood. They find prey animals at night by the sound of their breathing. They most often feed on cattle and horses, but occasionally attack sleeping humans.

Using heat sensors in its face, a vampire bat chooses a good spot to bite, where blood flows close to the surface. Then it makes a tiny cut in the animal's skin with its sharp teeth and licks up the blood that flows out. Its saliva contains **anticoagulants,** chemicals that keep the blood from clotting while they are feeding. The cuts don't usually harm the victim—or even wake it up!—but they can get infected. Vampire bats can also spread a deadly disease called rabies. So they are considered pests.

There are three species of vampire bats, and all live in the tropics or subtropics of Central and South America. Colonies of 100 to 1,000 bats live together. If a vampire bat goes without food for two nights in a row, it will starve to death. So others will spit up part of their meal to share with it. In return, they get a good grooming. The bats will also share meals with new mothers for the first two weeks after they give birth.

The sharp teeth on this vampire bat can slice into the skin of its prey.
Uwe Schmidt/Wikimedia Commons

Build Like a Beaver

Beavers build dams to block flowing water and create deeper pools. The deep water protects them from predators and keeps their lodges from freezing. They use their large rodent teeth to cut wood. They weave branches in place to hold back the water and seal them with mud and clay. Try making a beaver dam of your own. Can you build as well as a beaver?

MATERIALS

- 🖐 Sticks
- 🖐 Mud
- 🖐 Rocks
- 🖐 Paint tray

1. Use your sticks, mud, and rocks to make a dam in one corner of the paint tray. Try to make it watertight.

2. Pour water in the corner that you dammed off.

3. Observe: Does it hold water?

4. If your dam does not hold water, how could you make it better?

5. Test out your new design.

4

Home Sweet Home

No matter where you go, there's probably a mammal nearby. Mammals live on every continent except Antarctica and in every ocean. Some live in trees, some on land, and others in water. A few can even fly! Each mammal is specially adapted to survive in its habitat.

Under the Sea

Splash! A dolphin leaps out of the water. It looks like a fish, with its smooth body, fins, flippers, and tail, but it is actually a mammal. Like other mammals, it breathes air using lungs and feeds its babies milk. Most dolphins live in the ocean, but a few species can be found in rivers.

The mouflon is a type of wild sheep. *Alexas_Fotos/Pixabay*

Aquatic mammals have special adaptations to help them survive in their watery homes. Some live only in the water, while others, such as walruses, can haul themselves out onto the ice to rest and sunbathe. These animals are awkward on land—their flippers are not well suited for walking. But they are speedy and graceful in the water.

The sea otter lives on the Pacific coasts of North America and Asia. It spends almost all of its time in the water. Groups of otters lie on their backs or wrap themselves in long strands of kelp to sleep. The otter's ears and nostrils can close tightly to keep out water when it dives, so it doesn't have to worry about getting water up its nose.

The otter hunts for clams on the sea floor and brings them to the surface to eat. Then it floats on its back and bangs the shells against a stone on its stomach to crack them. The otter washes its paws and fur when it is done eating. This keeps its thick, oily fur in good condition.

Landlubbers

Humans live on land, and so do many other mammals. These "landlubbers" are also well adapted to their habitats. They have legs that are good for digging, running, climbing, or leaping.

Life Underground

Some mammals spend most of their lives underground. They come to the surface only rarely. The star-nosed mole is a digger extraordinaire. Its long claws act like shovels to help it burrow quickly into the soil. It hunts in ponds and streams as well as in its tunnels. The mole can't see well, but that's OK—it doesn't need to. The 22 fleshy tentacles on its nose help it find food in the dark. These tentacles are extremely sensitive—they have five times as many **neurons** as a human hand! When it finds a worm or insect, the mole gulps it down within a quarter of a second, making it the fastest eater in the world of mammals.

The naked mole rat is another amazing excavator. It may not win any beauty contests, but it can build elaborate underground kingdoms. Naked mole rats live in

A California sea otter naps in the water. Sea otters live in the ocean.
Bureau of Land Management/Flickr

colonies of about 80 animals. They feed on plant roots and create large systems of tunnels. The group is like a beehive, where only the queen produces young.

Out on a Limb

Tree-climbing mammals spend almost all of their time "out on a limb!" Their ability to climb trees lets these animals find fruits, berries, and leaves that others cannot reach. Trees also offer nesting spots that are safe from ground-dwelling predators.

Arboreal animals rarely come to the ground—they eat, make nests, and raise their young in trees. Three-toed sloths are a good example of this group. They only come to the ground once a week to poop. **Scansorial** mammals are good climbers. They may nest or find food on the ground but spend a lot of time in trees as well. Squirrels are in this group. They are good at scampering up and down trees.

Climbing mammals are well adapted to their treetop homes. Many have flexible hands or feet that can grasp branches, with long fingers or toes. These hook-like claws can lock into place. Animals that climb headfirst down trees often have special ankle bones that can turn so that their claws are reversed. This improves their grip and helps support their weight.

Many climbers, such as monkeys, have long, prehensile tails that help them hold onto branches as well. They can wrap their tail around a branch so it almost acts as another hand. Their long tails also help them balance. That's why tree squirrels have longer tails than their chipmunk cousins, which live on the ground. Climbing mammals also tend to have long arms for swinging from branch to branch, which is called **brachiation.**

Track Stars

Zoom! A cheetah speeds by. Cheetahs are the world's fastest land mammals, reaching speeds of up to 75 miles per hour over short distances. Many animals that live on land get around by running or walking. They have four long legs (or in the case of humans, two legs and two arms). Some, like cats and dogs, have padded paws with claws to help them grip the ground. Others, such as horses and antelope, have hooves on the ends of their feet to protect them.

Some mammals, including kangaroos, hares, and rodents, are better suited for jumping. These animals have long hind legs and shorter forelegs, with long tails that help them balance. In the case of the kangaroo, its tail acts as a third "leg" that helps to push it forward.

Taking Flight

The only mammals that can fly are the bats, but several other groups can glide long distances by spreading flaps of skin between their body and legs like a parachute. The sugar glider, for example, can soar the width of a football field. Its bushy tail helps it steer. This small marsupial lives in the forests of Australia, Indonesia, and New Guinea and rarely touches the ground.

Extreme Environments

Surviving in the desert can be tough! Food and water are hard to find, and the scorching heat makes it hard for a mammal to keep its body cool. On the other extreme, icy temperatures near the North and South Poles make it a challenge for animals to stay warm. Because fresh water is locked up in ice most of the year, it's hard to find water to drink there, so these areas are like deserts too—very, very cold ones. Let's look at some of the ways that mammals survive in these extreme environments.

A Long Winter's Sleep

It takes lots of energy for a mammal to keep its body warm in cold climates. Some animals get around this problem by hibernating. A hibernating mammal looks like it is sleeping. But its temperature drops dramatically, and its heart only beats a few times per minute. In this way, it uses very little energy to stay alive. Animals that **hibernate** must build up enough fat before winter so their bodies will not run out of energy by spring. Rodents often hibernate in their burrows, while bats cluster in caves for their long winter's sleep.

The Arctic ground squirrel wins the gold medal for longest hibernation—it sleeps in its cozy den for eight months, from September to April, slowing its heart rate to just one beat per minute while it sleeps. Its body temperature actually drops

The Arctic ground squirrel is a champion hibernator. *Bureau of Land Management/Flickr*

below freezing! The squirrel relies on a special brown fat to make enough heat to keep it alive.

Bears are what you might call "light hibernators." Their body temperature does not dip as low as that of many other hibernating animals. But bears do go into a deep sleep in winter, during which they do not eat, drink, or produce waste. This type of sleep is called **torpor.** Hibernating bears live off the fat they have stored up over the summer.

Bundle Up!

Mammals can be found even in the polar regions. While Antarctica has no land mammals, seals, whales, and other marine mammals can survive there. Polar mammals face extra challenges because of the extreme cold. They must keep their bodies from freezing even in subzero temperatures. Water is scarce too, because most of the fresh water is tied up in snow and ice.

Thick, shaggy fur keeps the Arctic fox warm when temperatures dip as low as −58° F (−50° C). It lies down and wraps its bushy tail around its body to keep its feet and face from freezing. Arctic foxes have much smaller ears than foxes that live in warmer climates. This cuts down on heat loss.

Polar marine mammals such as polar bears, seals, and whales rely on a thick layer of fat called **blubber** to keep them warm. A whale's blubber can be more than a foot thick! This dense fat acts like a warm winter coat. It also stores energy for use when food is scarce, and it helps the animal float. The blubber is different from the fat found in your body. It is thicker and has many more blood vessels in it than human body fat.

Warm as a Whale

Staying warm in the icy Arctic can be a challenge! Some Arctic mammals have a thick layer of fat called blubber to keep them warm. Try this experiment to see how well blubber works!

MATERIALS

- Pan of ice water
- Shortening

1. Prepare a pan of ice water.

2. Pick up a handful of shortening and pack it around one index finger. Make sure all of the skin is thickly covered.

3. Now dip both of your index fingers into the ice water. How cold does each one feel? Why do you think this is?

SPECIES SPOTLIGHT: Polar Bear

Polar bears are perfectly suited to the harsh Arctic climate. The polar bear's fur matches the snow and ice. Although it looks white because it reflects light, each hair is actually hollow and clear. Under the bear's fur is black skin that absorbs sunlight. This helps keep the bear warm. Beneath that, a thick layer of blubber provides additional insulation.

Scientists consider polar bears to be marine mammals because the majority of their food comes from the ocean. Several adaptations help polar bears hunt and get around in their icy environment. They are good swimmers. Webbing between the toes of their large, flat feet helps them swim. And a rough, nonslip surface helps the bears' feet keep their grip on slick ice.

Polar bears feed mainly on seals, along with the occasional whale **carcass** or walrus. They hunt by waiting near a seal's air hole until it comes up for air. Then they pounce!

Female polar bears dig dens in snow banks, where their cubs are born. A female usually gives birth to two cubs at one time but can have as many as four at once. The young stay with their mother for more than two years before they are ready to live on their own.

Today, climate change threatens polar bears' survival. Warming temperatures are causing sea ice to melt, break up, and move farther away from shore. Polar bears can be left stranded or have to swim hundreds of miles in search of food. Scientists estimate that two thirds of the polar bear population will die out by 2050.

A polar bear's rough paw pads help it grip the slippery ice. *Bering Land Bridge National Preserve/ Flickr*

Watch 'Em Sweat

Perspiration, or sweat, helps mammals cool their skin. As the water evaporates, it takes heat into the air with it. Find a friend and try this activity to see for yourself!

MATERIALS

- Water
- Small bowl
- Cotton swab
- Paper and pencil

1. Ask your friend to hold out both arms.

2. Put a tablespoon of water in the bowl.

3. Dip a swab in water and dab it on one of your friend's wrists.

4. Ask your friend to blow on both wrists. Which feels cooler? Write down your results.

5. Now switch places and try it on your own wrists.

The Arctic fox has small ears that reduce heat loss. The fennec fox's large ears help keep it cool in the desert.

Eric Kilby/Flickr

Staying Cool

Have you ever seen a dog panting on a hot day? Maybe you find yourself panting after a lot of exercise. Panting is one way that some desert animals, such as coyotes, get rid of extra heat. As they breathe over their tongues, water evaporates, taking heat with it. Desert animals often have large ears as well. Blood vessels in their ears are close to

Ryan Summers/Flickr

the surface, so the air can cool the blood, and that cooled blood circulates in the rest of the body.

Desert mammals don't waste a drop of water. In fact, the kangaroo rat does not need to drink at all. It gets a small amount of water from the food it eats. The kangaroo rat can also remove water from the air as it passes through its nostrils.

The camel can survive for six months without drinking. When it finds water, it can guzzle 30 gallons (113 L) in just 13 minutes! The camel's large hump stores fat that provides it with energy and water when needed.

Mammals that live in the desert tend to spend much of the day hiding from the hot sun. The white-throated wood rat builds itself a den inside a clump of prickly pear cactus, where it sleeps during the heat of the day. It comes out at night, when the air is cooler, to hunt for food. Larger mammals such as bighorn sheep can't burrow, but they find shady spots to rest during the hottest parts of the day.

A few desert mammals sleep for long periods of time to avoid weather that is too hot and dry. This sleep, which is similar to hibernation, is called **estivation**. Hedgehogs that live in deserts estivate during times of heat and drought.

Herds of reindeer migrate in winter to find food. *longtaildog/iStock*

Mammals on the Move

Whoosh! A herd of wildebeest thunders across the Serengeti Plain, leaving a cloud of dust in its wake. These African mammals travel up to 1,550 miles (2,500 km) to follow the rains. They give birth to their calves along the way. By the time they reach their destination, lush grasses greet them.

Traveling long distances to find food or better weather conditions is called migration. Not all mammals migrate, but many do, even if it is only moving to a higher or lower spot on a mountain. Those that can fly or swim tend to travel much farther than those that travel over land. Some hoofed mammals do travel long distances in search of food, however. Bison, zebras, elk, wildebeests, and antelope are a few examples. Elephants also travel a long way to find water.

Marine mammals often travel from the Arctic and Antarctic regions toward the equator in winter. The northern fur seal breeds on islands near Alaska. The males stay in the area all year, but the females travel all the way to California in winter. Their journey takes them around 3,000 miles (4,800 km).

These long-distance travelers have no maps to follow on their journey. So how do

Following the Clues

Some mammals migrate thousands of miles every year. Others travel only a short distance. They use different clues to find their way. These may be sounds, mental maps, etc. Try making a migration map of your own. Then see if your friends can follow the map to where X marks the spot!

MATERIALS
- Pencil
- Paper

1. Decide on your migration destination. Your path can be indoors or outdoors.

2. As you walk toward your destination, make notes along the way. What do you hear, see, and smell? Make sure these are not moving objects.

3. Draw a map of your migration route, marking these sights, sounds, and smells on the map.

4. Now give your map to a friend or family member and take them to where you started your journey. See if they can follow your map to the right location!

WORLD CHAMPION MIGRANTS

Caribou (sometimes called reindeer) hold the record for longest land migration among mammals. These elk-like creatures spend their winters in northern forests and summers on the **tundra**. They travel up to 3,100 miles (5,000 km) along the way, mostly walking but also swimming across inlets and lakes.

Whales are champion migrators as well. Recently, scientists tracked a female western gray whale that traveled 13,988 miles (22,511 km) in 172 days, swimming from the waters off Russia to Mexico and then back to Russia again. The previous record holder was the humpback whale, which travels up to 10,190 miles (16,400 km) from the Arctic or Antarctic to the equator and back again.

they find their way? Wildebeests follow the scent of rain, while others use visual landmarks such as mountains, rivers, and trees. Whales and dolphins follow landmarks on the ocean floor or along the coast. Other mammals rely on the position of the sun or the Earth's magnetic field.

Alien Invaders

Aliens are among us! No, not the kind from outer space. These aliens are species that were brought to new places either accidentally or on purpose, usually by humans. Most cannot survive in these new environments, but if conditions are just right, they can multiply and spread, especially if there are no natural predators there. These species can become pests and harm the ecosystems they invade by taking away resources from native species or even by eating them. We call these destructive newcomers **invasive species**.

One well-known invader is the nutria. Nutrias are semiaquatic mammals that are native to South America. They were brought to the United States around 1899 by farmers who planned to raise them and sell their fur. Some of the animals escaped or were set loose into the wild. Today, these ravenous rodents are destroying wetlands and crops in the southeastern United States. Some states are trying to control them by trapping or poisoning them. Some chefs have even come up with tasty recipes to encourage people to eat them!

5

Mammals Munch

Do you ever find yourself in front of the fridge, rummaging for something to eat? Many of us get our food from grocery stores or restaurants—we don't have to go out and hunt for it. Even our pets' food comes from the store. But finding food is a full-time job for mammals in the wild. No matter what they eat, they must always be on the lookout for their next meal. Some must avoid being eaten at the same time. Eating is serious business, and it's important to have the right tools for the job.

Grizzly bears graze on wild blueberries. *Denali National Park and Preserve/Flickr*

A Toothy Grin

Have you ever looked closely at your teeth in a mirror? They have different shapes. Your front teeth look like knife blades. They're good for pulling corn off the cob or biting into a cookie. Your canines are sharp and pointed, for piercing and gripping food. They can tear off a bite of steak. Your back teeth, or molars, are wide and flat. They grind food before you swallow it. Each kind of tooth has a different job. Having teeth that pull, grab, tear, and grind allows humans to be **omnivores**—we eat many different types of food, including plant parts such as leaves, grains, fruit, roots, and nuts, as well as meat from animals. We need more than one sort of tooth because we need to quickly swallow our food so we can breathe.

Mammals are the only animals that have different types of teeth with different jobs. Reptiles, fish, and amphibians have just one kind of tooth. Mammals are also the only animals that start off with milk teeth, or baby teeth. The milk teeth fall out and are replaced with permanent teeth as the animal grows.

GOLD-MEDAL MAMMALS

If a mammal Olympics were held, who would win the gold in each event? Check out this list of champions!

Largest mammal: Blue whale

Smallest mammal: Bumblebee bat (length) and Etruscan shrew (mass)

Largest mammal to build a nest: Gorilla

Fastest eater: Star-nosed mole

Fastest 100-meter dash: Cheetah

Slowest heartbeat: Blue whale

Largest eyes (for its size): Philippine tarsier

Densest fur: Sea otter

Longest average migration: Humpback whale

Noisiest land mammal: Howler monkey

Eat or Be Eaten

Living things in an ecosystem can be organized by what they eat, or their place in the food chain. Ecologists call these groupings **trophic levels**. Plants are the **producers** in an ecosystem because they make their own food by absorbing energy from the sun.

The next levels are called **consumers**. Primary consumers, or herbivores, get their energy by eating plants. This group includes grazing animals such as deer, rabbits, and bison as well as animals that eat fruits, leaves, seeds, and berries, such as fruit bats and koalas.

The secondary consumers are animals that feed on herbivores. They may feed on plants as well. Tertiary, or third-level, consumers feed on secondary consumers. Some of these are eaten by still larger animals, but some are apex predators. **Apex predators** have no natural enemies other than humans (and parasites)—they are at the top of the food chain. Examples of these are wolves and killer whales.

There are two other layers in a trophic pyramid. **Scavengers** such as hyenas eat carrion—dead or decaying animals. **Decomposers** are organisms such as fungi and bacteria that break down organic material. They bring the energy full cycle and return

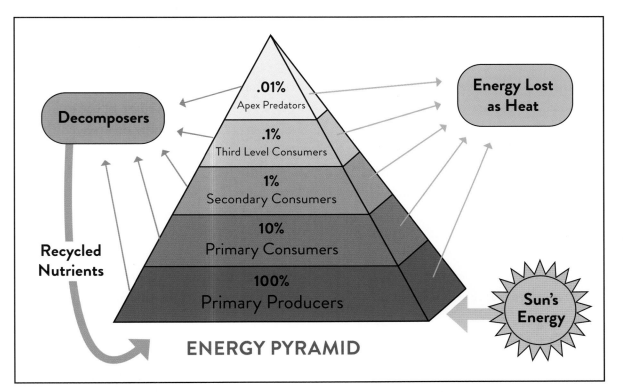

.01%
Apex Predators

.1%
Third Level Consumers

1%
Secondary Consumers

10%
Primary Consumers

100%
Primary Producers

ENERGY PYRAMID

Decomposers

Recycled Nutrients

Energy Lost as Heat

Sun's Energy

This energy pyramid shows the flow of energy through the trophic levels in an ecosystem.

A lion's teeth are perfect for killing prey and tearing off hunks of meat to eat. *AjayLalu/ Pixabay*

it to the soil. They do this by breaking it down into smaller and smaller bits so that the nutrients can again be used by plants.

Feasting on Meat

Grrr! A lion tears off a large chunk of meat from a freshly caught antelope carcass, then gulps it down. The lion is well adapted for this carnivorous lifestyle. Its long canine teeth and sharp claws help it stab and hang

onto its prey, just as a housecat does with a mouse. Once it has killed a prey animal, it uses its carnassial teeth to slice off pieces of flesh to eat. These back teeth sharpen each other as the animal eats by rubbing against each other like knife sharpeners. If you've ever seen a dog gnawing on a bone with the side of its mouth, you've seen carnassial teeth in action.

Like the lion, most carnivores have sharp teeth that can grip and slice into

their prey. They can tear away meat and even crack and crush bones. A carnivore's gut is short and simple, because meat is easier to digest than plants.

Not all carnivores have long, sharp teeth, though. Some have no teeth at all! The pangolin, for example, uses its long, sticky tongue to pull ants or termites from their mounds. Grit (small rocks and sand) sticks to the animal's tongue when it reaches into the soil. This grit helps to grind up the insects in its stomach.

The humpback whale is another predator that lacks sharp teeth. Its diet mainly consists of shrimplike krill and small fish such as sardines. It sucks in these prey animals with a mouthful of water and pushes the water back out through a filter-like structure called baleen. The fish and krill are trapped inside its mouth and swallowed.

Teaming Up

What do you do when the animal you want to eat is larger than you? Teaming up can be a good strategy. While most predators hunt alone, some, such as wolves, wild dogs, chimpanzees, hyenas, bottlenose dolphins, and orcas, work together to bring down prey. These are called pack hunters or social predators.

Wolves live and hunt in large groups called packs. The top male and female are called the alpha pair. The pack works together to surround and attack its prey. In this way, wolves can bring down even very large animals, such as elk or bison, that they might not be able to kill on their own. Each wolf gets a share of the food, and some is taken back to the den to feed the pups.

Chimpanzees work together to hunt monkeys. They first patrol the area, scanning the treetops and listening carefully for their prey. When a monkey is located, a group of chimpanzees climbs the tree to attack it. The hunters share the meat with each other and often with others in the group.

A zebra's sharp, flat teeth are good for grazing.
hammett79/iStock

TRY THIS!

Fridge Food Chain

What's in your food chain? Take a peek in your refrigerator to find out.

MATERIALS

- 20 items from your refrigerator or freezer
- Pen or pencil
- Sheet of paper

1. With an adult's help, choose 20 random items from your refrigerator or freezer.

2. Look at the ingredient label of each one.

3. Where does the main ingredient fall in the trophic pyramid? Is it a producer (plant)? Is it an herbivore (for example, beef)? Is it an omnivore (for example, pig or chicken)? A carnivore? A decomposer (for example, a mushroom)?

4. Draw a trophic pyramid on your paper like the one shown on page 43.

5. List your food items in the appropriate section of the pyramid.

HOW DO MAMMALS HELP?

What would a world without mammals look like? While we might be happy to get rid of some pest species, like the Norway rat, every animal plays an important role in its ecosystem. Mammals' food choices often play a part in the benefits they provide. For example, oak trees often sprout where squirrels bury acorns, so a world without squirrels might have fewer trees. Bats, lemurs, sugar gliders, and other small mammals also pollinate flowers, and many mammals carry seeds that stick to their coats or are dropped in their poop. The mammal "clean-up crew" of scavengers such as the Virginia opossum helps remove carrion that might otherwise spread disease.

A less obvious but no less important job of mammals is population control. Scientists are still learning about the complex ways that predators, prey, and plants interact. A study in Yellowstone National Park showed this clearly. After wolves were reintroduced to the park in 1995, amazing changes began to happen. Earlier, with no wolves, elk overgrazed the park. When the wolves returned, they preyed on the elk and kept them on the move. With fewer elk browsing, trees began to grow back. Beavers returned to the park, building dams and creating new habitat for fish. Streams cleared and songbirds returned. Almost every aspect of the ecosystem was renewed, all because one missing piece—the wolf—was put back in place.

Eat Your Veggies

Animals that eat only plants, such as deer and bison, are called herbivores. Their teeth and jaws are adapted for grazing or browsing on plants. Their sharp front teeth can easily snip off plant stems. Flat molars in the back grind and crush the food. Beavers can eat even tough, woody bark and branches.

The panda lives in the forests of China, where it feeds mainly on bamboo. Its specially shaped thumbs help it hold onto the bamboo stems. It can eat up to $\frac{1}{10}$ its weight in bamboo each day! The panda's strong jaws and teeth crush the tough twigs.

Plant cell walls are made of cellulose, which makes plants woody and tough. These cells are much harder to break down than softer animal cells. Fortunately, an herbivore's gut is specially designed to deal with this problem. Many herbivorous mammals have a pouch in their gut called a rumen where bacteria can break down the plant material. Hoofed mammals such as cows, camels, and goats do not completely chew up their food up before swallowing it. Instead, they bring it up from their rumen later to chew it some more before swallowing it again. This clump of partially digested food is called cud. Animals that produce cud are called ruminants.

Eating It All

How does a fresh slice of pepperoni pizza sound right now? The combination of vegetables, grains, meat, and cheese makes it perfect for an omnivore. Omnivores can eat both plants and animals, and even algae and fungi. This is an advantage because they can adapt to changes in the environment. If there is no meat available, they can eat more plants, and vice versa.

Many mammals are omnivores, including humans (although some people choose not to eat meat), raccoons, pigs, bears, skunks, monkeys, and rats. The largest omnivore found on land is the Kodiak bear, a type of grizzly bear that lives in Alaska. Like

Become a Tooth Sleuth

An animal's teeth give clues to how and what it eats. See if you can solve the mystery!

- ✋ Pictures of mammal skulls
- ✋ Pencil

1. Ask an adult to print off some photos of mammal skulls from the Internet. They should lightly write the name of the animal on the back of the paper, along with what it eats.

2. Without looking at the back of the paper, look carefully at the animal's skull—specifically, its teeth. Compare them to the image below to determine what kind of teeth they are: canines, incisors, molars, or premolars. How are they arranged?

3. Guess what this animal might eat based on the type of teeth it has.

4. Now look at the back of the paper. Was your answer correct? If not, can you figure out where you went wrong?

5. Try this on a friend and test their sleuthing abilities!

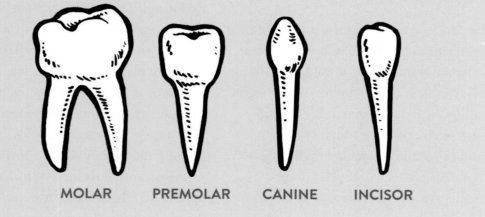

MOLAR PREMOLAR CANINE INCISOR

other bears, it eats a wide variety of foods. Omnivores are an important part of the food chain in natural systems. They keep both vegetation and smaller animals in check.

Omnivores tend to have sharp, pointed teeth to tear meat as well as flat molars to crush plants. An omnivore's gut can digest both meat and plant material. But it does not break down plants as well as an herbivore's digestive system does. So tougher materials, such as cellulose and fiber, exit as waste.

The Deader the Better

Does a fresh piece of roadkill make you say, "Yum!"? Probably not, since you're not a scavenger. For some animals, however, that smelly morsel would be an appealing feast. Scavengers are animals that feed on dead or decaying plant or animal material. For mammals, this often means eating carrion. The hyena, for example, likes to feed on meat from other animals' kills. However, packs of hyenas hunt antelope or other animals when needed, so they are also considered carnivores. Their strong jaws can crush bones.

The Virginia opossum is a common scavenger in North America. It is attracted to dead animals and can often be spotted feeding on roadkill at night. Carrion does not make up its whole diet, however.

Opossums also eat fruit, nuts, and grass and will hunt small animals such as mice, birds, insects, and snakes. They also keep gardens clear of slugs, snails, and ticks.

Going Hungry

What happens when food is scarce? Some mammals can switch to another food source. But others simply go hungry. The Canada lynx lives in northern forests and feeds mainly on snowshoe hares. When hares are plentiful, it eats about two hares every three days. When it cannot find enough hares, it will eat other small animals such as mice, squirrels, ptarmigans (a small bird), and even carrion. However, these food sources do not supply all the lynx's nutritional needs, so without enough hares, the lynx may starve or become diseased.

About every ten years, the hare population grows too large and crashes as some of the animals starve. With fewer hares to eat, the lynx population shrinks as well. Then, with fewer predators and less competition for food, the hare population begins to grow again. With more hares to eat, the lynx population begins to grow again, too. The two animals are locked into this cycle together.

Spotted hyenas are scavengers that feed on other animals' kills. *tonyo_au/Pixabay*

The Canada lynx feeds on snowshoe hares.
Denali National Park and Preserve/Flickr

SPECIES SPOTLIGHT: Tiger

The world's largest cat species is the tiger, which lives in forests, swamps, and grasslands in parts of Asia. The Siberian tiger can reach 10 feet (3 m) in length, while other species are a little smaller. Tigers rest during the day by sleeping in the shade or in a pool of water. At night, they come out to hunt. They stalk deer, wild cattle, and wild pigs, but will eat any kind of meat. Sick or wounded tigers may even attack humans. Tigers that acquire a taste for humans are called maneaters.

The tiger's good eyesight and hearing help it find food. It sneaks up on a prey animal, rushes, and pounces, killing the animal with its teeth and claws. The tiger may take several days to finish off the meal, eating up to 60 pounds (27 kg) in a single night.

Female tigers give birth to a litter of two to four cubs every two to three years. The cubs are the size of large kittens. They drink their mother's milk for about six months, but by two months of age they start eating meat as well.

Unlike your housecat, tigers often swim. *272447/Pixabay*

Leftovers for Lunch

Some mammals avoid food supply problems by storing food. A leopard can chow down 22 pounds (10 kg) of meat in a single meal, but its stomach is not big enough to hold a whole antelope. Rather than letting scavengers steal and eat its kill, the leopard hoists the carcass into a tree. There it can feast on leftovers for days while circling hyenas go hungry.

Arctic foxes store food as well. They mainly feed on lemmings, birds, and eggs. They create caches of dead animals and eggs that can feed them for months when food is scarce. The fox has a good memory and can remember where its food is stored.

Find a Food Chain

What mammals live in your area? What do they eat? In this activity, you will research a local mammal's food chain and learn what food sources it relies on.

MATERIALS

- Books or Internet access
- Pens, markers, colored pencils
- Poster board

1. Choose a mammal that lives in your area. It can be an herbivore, omnivore, carnivore, or scavenger. If you're not sure what mammals live in your area, check the library or the Internet.

2. Now look for more details about your animal. What does it eat? What preys on it?

3. Do the same for any other animals in the food chain.

4. Now draw your mammal's food chain on a sheet of poster board. Start with the producers (plants), followed by the primary, secondary, and tertiary consumers. What decomposers might feed on these animals when they die?

5. Can you identify any threats to the survival of this mammal in your area?

6

The Web of Life

All living things, including mammals, are part of the web of life. They are connected to each other in many ways. When something happens to one kind of animal, it affects others—sometimes in unexpected ways.

Offense or Defense?

Do you like to play or watch games like soccer or basketball? Sometimes players play offense—pushing forward to score points. Other times they play defense, trying to stop the other team from scoring points.

The northern tamandua is a type of anteater. *phototrip/iStock*

For mammals, however, these offense and defense roles are not a game. They are a matter of life and death. Some mammals are predators. They're on the offense—hunting other animals for food. Some mammals are prey. They must always play defense, hiding from predators to survive. Many mammals fall into both categories—they hunt smaller animals but are also hunted by larger ones. No matter which "team" they're on, mammals are in a constant battle for survival.

Nature's Balancing Act

To us, it might seem cruel for a coyote to kill a rabbit, or for a cat to kill a mouse. But we don't think twice when bats gobble up insects or a bison nibbles grass. The truth is, none of these animals is "good" or "bad" for finding the food it needs to survive. It's all part of nature's balancing act.

All parts of the ecosystem are necessary to keep the system in balance. If there are too few predators, herbivores will **overpopulate** and overgraze the area, leaving it bare and dry. Then they will run out of food and starve. If there are too few herbivores, predators will starve. Both are needed to keep the ecosystem stable. In addition, by mainly hunting the old and sickly animals that are

easiest to catch, predators can actually help their prey populations stay healthier.

Hide and Seek

Although they aren't as colorful as birds or insects, mammals come in a variety of colors and patterns. Sometimes their appearance helps to camouflage them. Fur or skin that matches the environment helps an animal hide from predators or sneak up on prey without being seen. For example, the white fur of a polar bear matches the snow.

Tigers have stripes that blend in with the grasslands where they live. And the spots on a white-tailed deer fawn help to hide it while its mother hunts for food.

Many mammals are darker on top and lighter underneath. This type of camouflage is called **countershading**. It makes the animal harder to see from above because it is the same shade as the ground. Seen from below, its lighter underside blends in with the sky. Animals that live in water often show countershading. But many land

A speckled fawn curls up in the grass. Its spots help hide it from predators. *JillWellington/Pixabay*

animals do too. In addition to making the animal harder for flying predators to see, scientists believe the darker color also helps to protect it from too much ultraviolet light, which can damage skin.

Super Speed

A rabbit has few defenses against predators. Its first trick is to freeze and try to blend in with the background. If that fails, it uses its long legs to speed away. It can reach speeds of up to 35 miles per hour (56 kph) over a short distance—not fast enough to outrun every predator, but faster than many. It also uses a zigzag path that makes it harder to catch.

This zigzag trick works for zebras and impalas on the African savanna as well. Even though lions and cheetahs have more muscle power and speed, they are only successful at catching their prey about a third of the time. This is because their prey have special ankle bones with very deep grooves. They can slow down and turn sharply before the predator can react. This gives the prey animals an advantage.

Warning Signs

If you see an animal with black and white stripes, stay back! Mammals with black

SPECIES SPOTLIGHT: Zebra

Is it black with white stripes, or white with black stripes? In most cases, scientists say, zebras are white with black stripes, because their bellies are usually white. However, some zebras show the opposite pattern, and underneath all those stripes is black skin.

Scientists aren't sure exactly what purpose a zebra's stripes serve, but they may help camouflage it or even act as a natural sunscreen. They may also help keep biting flies away by confusing them. Amazingly, no two zebras' stripes are exactly alike, and they may be able to recognize each other's stripes. The three different species of zebras have stripes of different widths.

Zebras spend their days grazing on grasses and traveling to find food and water. They live in family groups on the plains of Africa. These family groups may join together to form large herds.

Baby zebras, called foals, are soft and fuzzy, and their stripes appear brown. A zebra foal recognizes its mother by her stripes. It can walk just 20 minutes after it is born. This is important, because it must keep up with its mother and the rest of the herd.

A zebra and foal graze.
idahronn79/Flickr

Why Are Polar Bears White?

Camouflage helps both predators and their prey. It helps prey animals hide from predators. It also helps predators sneak up on their prey. Try this activity with a friend to see how it works.

MATERIALS

- Several types of paper (newspaper, magazines, construction paper, tracing paper, wax paper, wrapping paper, etc.)
- Scissors
- Large sheet of newspaper with some color ads
- Timer

1. Using scissors and the outline shown, cut out 10 bear heads from different colors and types of paper.

2. Spread out a sheet of newspaper. Lay the bears out on the newspaper.

3. Set the timer for ten seconds. See how many bears your friend can find and pick up before the time is up.

4. Switch places and try finding the bears yourself.

5. Which patterns were easiest to find? Which were hardest?

The skunk's black and white stripes warn predators to stay away. If threatened, it will spray a smelly fluid from its tail end. *JeremyRichards/iStock*

and white fur, such as skunks, often give off bad-smelling or toxic chemicals. Since many of them are active at night, the white stripes help make them more visible. The pattern warns predators to stay away. A skunk's musk contains sulfur, a chemical that gives it a burning, rotten-egg smell. When the skunk is threatened, it gives a warning signal by arching its back and stamping its feet. If the predator persists, the skunk can spray smelly fluid up to 12 feet (3.7 m) away. Most predators who meet a skunk are not eager to meet another!

Escape Mode

Mammals use many different tricks to escape from danger. One of these is pretending to be dead. This behavior, called **thanatosis,** can save an animal's life. The opossum, for example, falls over unconscious when it is threatened. Its body stiffens, its breathing slows, its mouth falls open, and it gives off an odor from its anal glands. This makes the opossum smell like a dead, rotting carcass. A predator that prefers live food will turn up its nose and move on. An opossum can stay in this condition for up to four hours.

Spiny animals like the porcupine rely on prickly quills to keep predators away. When a predator approaches, a porcupine rattles its hollow tail quills and raises its tail. The needlelike quills on its body are covered with tiny barbs. If the predator gets too close, it will get a painful surprise. The quills slide easily into the predator's skin, but the barbs make them very hard to pull out. The wounds may cause infection or even death.

The nine-banded armadillo is one tough cookie. It looks like an armored tank. Bony plates called scutes cover its sides and back, so when danger is near, it digs a trench and huddles down to hide its soft belly. Few predators can bite through its tough armor.

Fighting Back

Some mammals turn vicious when danger appears. Mammals use their teeth, claws, horns, and hooves to fight back however they can.

The moose is a large member of the deer family that can reach 7 feet (2.1 m) in height and 1,300 pounds (600 kg). A

TRY THIS!

Write a Putrid Poem

Some mammals, like the skunk, sloth, and hyena, smell . . . well . . . putrid. Read more about why these animals stink, and then write a humorous poem about one of them. The more putrid your prose, the better! Here are a couple examples to get you started.

Sloth

Is that a moth,
Mr. Sloth,
in your squirming,
stinking suit?

Skunk

Stamp, stamp! Stay away!
Or I'll let loose and spray.
Uh-oh, I warned you!
PSST!

(left) **The porcupine's sharp quills protect it from predators.** *rixonline/iStock*

(right) **A bull moose uses its antlers to defend itself and its territory.** *PublicDomainImages/ Pixabay*

moose's massive size makes it intimidating enough, but its huge pair of antlers adds to its danger. These large bony structures found on male moose can reach 6 feet (1.8 m) in width. They can be used as shields or weapons in battle, and also help attract mates. Moose lose their antlers after mating season is over and grow them again in the spring.

It's rare to find a venomous mammal, but there are a few. The slow loris lives in the forests of several Asian countries. Glands in its elbows produce venom, a poisonous liquid. The animal licks its elbow and the venom mixes with its saliva, creating a venomous bite. Slow lorises sometimes lick their young before going off to forage, making them poisonous to any predator that might stop by for a snack. Other venomous mammals are the platypus, vampire bats, and some shrews, moles, and solenodons.

Safety in Numbers

Hoofed mammals often hang out in large groups, or herds. This has many advantages. The herd works together to spot danger. Each animal is less likely to be singled out this way, and predators may be afraid to attack a whole herd for fear of being trampled. Antelope herds once contained up to 10 million animals; today they are much smaller but still number in the thousands.

The musk ox's horns and powerful hooves make any predator think twice about attacking it. But young animals are easier to pick off. So, when a predator comes near, adults form a circle around their young, horns facing out. Most predators will back off when faced with a wall of large, angry musk oxen.

Some predators hunt in groups too. Beaked dolphins, for example, will work together to herd fish into groups called "bait balls," then take turns plowing through the swirling mass to chow down. Packs of African wild dogs work together to chase an antelope or wildebeest until it gets tired, then attack its nose and underside until it collapses. The dogs fill their stomachs and then return to the den to regurgitate some meat for the pups and any weak or ill members that stayed behind.

WORLD'S MOST DANGEROUS MAMMALS

Surprisingly, one of the world's most dangerous mammals (to humans) is also known as "man's best friend"—the dog. While dogs can make wonderful pets, they do sometimes attack and even kill humans. In the United States alone, 4.5 million dog bites occur every year. While the majority of these are not fatal, around one in five bites becomes infected. Dogs can also carry a deadly disease called rabies.

The hippopotamus may look slow, but it moves quickly in water and is aggressive toward intruders. Between 500 and 3,000 people are killed by hippos every year. It is thought that they may mistake small boats for crocodiles and attack them.

Lions kill around 100 people every year, while tigers kill 50 to 250 people annually in the Sundarbans. About the same number of people are killed in the United States every year by horses. Most of these are from riding accidents.

Around 100 to 500 people are killed by elephants each year. Some are gored by elephant tusks, while others are trampled when they get in an elephant's way.

Other Relationships

Mammals don't just relate to each other as food sources. Some have more complex relationships. When at least one organism benefits from a relationship, it is called **symbiosis**. There are three different types of symbiosis.

Mutualism

Sometimes a relationship is good for both parties. They help each other out. This type of symbiosis is called **mutualism**. Several African mammals including elephants, zebras, rhinos, and Cape buffalo have a mutualistic relationship with a bird called the oxpecker. The bird lands on these animals' backs and feeds on ticks and insects it finds there. The mammals benefit from this cleaning service as well.

Warthogs and mongooses have a similar relationship. A warthog will lie down and allow the mongoose to pick off ticks and insects. Again, both benefit—the mongoose

An oxpecker perches on the back of an impala. It feeds on ticks and insects that it finds there. *IanZA/Pixabay*

gets an easy meal and the warthog gets rid of those itchy pests.

Coyotes and badgers make an unusual pair, but they sometimes team up to hunt. Both hunt ground squirrels and prairie dogs on the grasslands. The coyote chases them above ground, and the badger waits in a burrow to catch them if they return. Only one of the pair will get a meal, but over time, both predators catch more prey by working together than they would on their own.

Commensalism

A **commensal** relationship benefits one member of the pair, but doesn't affect the other one at all. An example of this is the great egret, which follows herds of cattle to feed on the insects they stir up. The egret benefits from the extra food, but its presence does not help or hurt the cattle.

Another example of commensalism is the golden jackal. If this wolflike animal is shunned by its pack, it follows a tiger and feeds on food that the tiger leaves behind. This doesn't bother the tiger, but doesn't help it either. Barnacles and whales have a commensal relationship too. Barnacles are small sea animals related to crabs. They attach themselves to the skin of a

whale. These crusty passengers do not hurt the whale, but they get a free ride to new sources of food.

Parasitism

Have you ever found a flea or tick on a pet? These are parasites. **Parasitism** is a relationship that helps one member and hurts the other. Fleas and ticks live on the outside of the body. But parasites can live inside the body too. Various types of worms and protozoa can make animals sick. For example, heartworms live in the heart, lungs, and blood vessels of dogs, cats,

LOOK FOR

Make a Tracking Station

Who visits your yard when you're not around? Try this activity to find out.

MATERIALS
- Board, about 2 feet x 2 feet (60 cm x 60 cm)
- Flour, cornmeal, sand, or dirt
- Empty tuna can
- Peanut butter, cereal, birdseed, or a small piece of raw meat
- Field guide to animal tracks (optional)
- Internet access (optional)

1. Lay a board on the ground outdoors. Sprinkle the top with flour, cornmeal, sand, or dirt.

2. Choose one of the food items to place in the tuna can.

3. Set the can in the middle of the board.

4. Check your board in the morning. Use a field guide or the Internet to identify any animal tracks.

and some wild mammals. Without treatment, the animal host may die.

Mammals have various ways to keep parasites away. Some groom each other. Others try to remove parasites on their own. For instance, African elephants use their tails and pick up twigs to brush away biting flies. These parasites feed on the elephant's blood. Animals can treat internal parasites on their own too. For instance, baboons eat the leaves of a certain plant to kill flatworms. Pregnant lemurs eat the leaves and bark of tamarind and fig trees to treat parasites.

7

Life Goes On

Along with finding food and staying safe, mammals spend a lot of time finding mates and caring for their young. This **instinct** helps their species survive.

Love Is in the Air

Humans aren't the only mammals who sing love songs! Male mice whistle a tune to attract mates. This sound is too high-pitched for humans to hear. Male  bowhead whales hum a low, complex song. Whatever their methods, mammals spend a lot of time and energy wooing mates and raising their young. It's an important job—if members of a species do not produce young, their kind will eventually die out.

A seal pup nuzzles its mother. *272447/Pixabay*

Finding a Mate

Love can make people do strange things. Being in love—or looking for love—affects the way we walk, talk, and act. Attraction affects the way other mammals look and behave as well.

Male mammals often have special behaviors that help them attract mates. These are called **courtship** behaviors. And when it comes to looks, males tend to be showier too. There's a good reason for that. Female mammals usually have several males to choose from, so males must compete for their attention. Females prefer males with lots of energy, strength, and "good looks"—whatever that means to a mouse or meerkat or mongoose. These things show that the male is in good health and will pass on good genes. Choosing the fittest males makes a female's offspring more likely to survive.

Some of these courtship displays may seem odd to us. But then again, buying flowers and chocolate might sound strange to a hooded seal! The male of this species puffs up part of his nose to create a big pink balloon on his face in order to impress the females. He also has a sac in his nose that can inflate like a hood over his face. Male walruses clack their teeth, whistle, and

 TRY THIS!

Follow Your Nose

Can you follow a scent trail as well as a bloodhound? Grab a friend and try this activity to find out!

MATERIALS

- Bandanna
- Perfume, vanilla, or other scent

1. Get permission from a teacher or parent to use a room for this activity and ask for help making sure there's nothing left out that could be badly stained by the perfume or other scent that you're going to use for this activity.

2. Use the bandanna to blindfold your friend and take them to the chosen room.

3. Walk around the room and dab a drop of perfume or other scent every few feet along your path to create a scent trail.

4. Now take off the blindfold and see if your friend can follow the trail.

5. Switch places and try the activity for yourself. Use a different scent so you don't get mixed up.

make bell-like sounds to attract the watching females. Male humpback dolphins pick up sponges and offer them to prospective mates.

Another way mammals find and attract mates is by giving off chemicals called **pheromones**. These invisible signals help males and females find each other. They can show when a female is in heat—ready to mate. A male dog can smell a female in heat from more than half a mile (1 km) away.

Punch! Kick! Thud! No, this isn't a boxing match, although it looks like one. Male kangaroos literally come to blows at mating time. One will end up as the most dominant male. He will mate with all the females in the group.

Male deer also fight during mating season. They lock antlers and shove each other until one is forced back and runs off. Males can be injured during this shoving match, sometimes permanently.

No Trespassing

Did you ever see a dog stop to pee on every fence post and fire hydrant it passes? In between, it sniffs the ground energetically.

The dog is marking its territory—the area it has claimed as its own. When it sniffs the ground, it is reading the signals left by other dogs. Mammals often use scents to mark their territory, especially when it comes to mating time. Antelope, for instance, have glands in front of their eyes that produce scent. They rub this scent on grass and twigs at the edge of their territory. Antelope also use feces and urine to mark their boundaries.

Scent marking is the most common way that mammals mark their territory, but it is not the only way. Male and female white-cheeked gibbons use loud songs to mark their territory. They sing a 10-minute-long duet at sunrise to warn other gibbons away. Male white rhinos mark their territory with piles of dung, which they scrape around with their feet. Other rhinos can both see and smell these piles.

Black bears rub their scent on trees, but also claw and bite them to make visual marks on the tree. Whatever their method, all these signs say "Keep out! No trespassing!"

It Starts with an Egg

Every mammal starts off as an egg inside its mother's body. This egg is not like the ones you might see on your breakfast plate—it is a tiny, single cell. Even a giant whale starts off as a speck! The egg is in its mother's uterus. Once a male and female have mated and sperm has joined the egg, the cell starts dividing. As it grows into an embryo, an umbilical cord forms to connect the developing baby to the placenta. The embryo receives nutrients and oxygen from the placenta through the umbilical cord. A sac

The white rhino uses piles of dung to mark its territory. *greatplaces360/Pixabay*

of fluid surrounds the developing baby and cushions it. Once the embryo begins to take shape, it is known as a fetus.

The fetus grows inside the mother's uterus until it is ready to be born (except in monotremes, which lay eggs). It takes about nine months for a human baby to develop inside its mother. This time is called the gestation period. Some mammals have an even longer gestation period. A female elephant carries its baby for 22 months—that's almost two years!

Smaller mammals have more litters, give birth more often, and raise their young much faster than larger mammals. Rabbits are famously fast breeders—a single female can birth 60 or more babies per year. However, many of these bunnies do not reach adulthood because they die of disease or starvation, or are eaten by predators such as foxes and owls.

Marsupials also have a short gestation time. They are born before they are able to survive out in the open. Instead, the tiny babies crawl to their mother's pouch or abdomen and latch onto a nipple. Kangaroos and many other marsupials stay in the pouch, nursing for weeks or even months until their body is more developed, thanks to their mom's milk. When the joey comes out of the pouch, it is about as developed as other mammals are when they are born.

Happy Birthday!

When a baby mammal is born, its mother licks it clean. This helps to prevent infections and avoids attracting predators to the scent of blood. This spit bath also helps the pair to bond. If a baby is taken away before the mother has a chance to lick it, the

A young Barbary macaque hitches a ride.
blickpixel/Pixabay

mother may not recognize the baby later or accept it as her own. This all happens by instinct—the mother does it automatically, without thinking.

The baby has instincts as well. Its first task is to find its mother's teat and latch on to suckle. (Or in the case of monotremes, it clings to her fur and laps up milk that oozes from pores in her skin.) The baby has a strong sucking reflex that ensures it will get enough food. A baby mammal feeds on its mother's milk for days, weeks, months, or even years. Milk is mostly water, but it also contains fats, carbohydrates, proteins, vitamins, and minerals. The amount of each nutrient in the milk varies depending on the baby's needs. Human breast-milk contains about 3–5 percent fat. A black rhino's watery milk is only about

RABBIT MATH

Rabbits are known for multiplying quickly. A female European rabbit gives birth to 1 to 14 babies at a time, and she can get pregnant again within days of giving birth. She can breed monthly, beginning at about 8 months of age, and can live for up to 9 years. In nature, predators and disease keep the population of rabbits from getting too high and doing damage to their environment. But what if they didn't? How many offspring could a single rabbit produce in its lifetime? Try some rabbit math!

If one rabbit gives birth to an average of six young per litter and has 10 litters per year, she has 60 babies at the end of year one. If half of those are females, she has 30 daughters.

In year two, the rabbit has another 60 babies. Her daughters each have 60 babies as well. So by the end of the year, there are $31 \times 60 = 1,860$ baby rabbits. Including the original 31 females, there are 961 females.

The following year, these 961 females each give birth to 60 babies. Now there are 57,660 young, or 28,830 females plus the previous 961, for a total of 29,791 females.

In year four, those females give birth to 60 babies each, for a total of 893,730 females, bringing the total to 923,521 females, or 1,847,042 rabbits overall.

As you can see, that original rabbit pair produced nearly 2 million bunnies, including the males, in just four years. That's some serious rabbit math!

0.2 percent fat, while a hooded seal's is 60 percent fat. Young seals need to gain weight quickly and develop a thick layer of blubber before winter comes. The tammar wallaby's milk is 14 percent sugar—one of the most sugary milks around. The eastern cottontail rabbit's milk has the most protein, at 15 percent. This protein-rich milk helps the baby go a long time between feedings while its mother is out foraging for food.

As the baby grows, its mother's body makes more milk to supply its needs. But

SPECIES SPOTLIGHT: Orangutan

An orangutan swings through the forests of Sumatra and Borneo. This large ape has shaggy red hair. Its name means "person of the forest" in the Malay language. A male orangutan is about five feet tall, and his arms stretch seven feet wide. Females are smaller. An orangutan's hands nearly reach the ground when it is standing. Its strong arms help it swing from branch to branch through the treetops, where it spends most of its time.

Orangutans find most of their food in the treetops. They mainly feed on fruit but will also eat leaves, honey, insects, and bird eggs. They even sleep in trees, making new nests each night and using leaves as umbrellas or even as ponchos.

A female orangutan gives birth every eight years, and cares for her baby for six to seven years. Females sometimes gather in groups while their young play together. Adult males live on their own and make loud calls to keep other males away from their territory. When they fight, they charge each other and bite each other's cheek pads and ears.

Because orangutans rely on forests to survive, they are threatened by logging and other human activities such as hunting and **poaching**. Their forests are being replaced by palm oil plantations and other farming operations. If things do not change, scientists estimate orangutans may be extinct within the next decade.

Male orangutans have large cheek pads. *Eric Kilby/Flickr*

eventually, the young animal needs more than just milk to grow. The young mammal begins to eat other food along with the milk. Soon, it will be weaned. It will stop drinking milk entirely and eat other foods instead.

Growing Up

How many baby teeth have you lost? Losing baby teeth to make room for larger permanent teeth is just one way that mammals change as they grow. Most mammals look like mini versions of their parents when they are born (except marsupials, which look more like jelly beans!). But they do go through changes as they grow. Their body shape changes as they grow larger. When they reach a certain age, their bodies start producing special **hormones.** These chemicals circulate in the bloodstream, and some cause mammals' bodies to develop in new ways in order to be able to reproduce. This stage is called **puberty**. After they become adults, these young mammals will begin looking for mates and getting ready to become parents themselves. This takes longer in some species than in others. Female mice are adults and able to give birth when they are only 6 weeks old. Elephants, on the other hand, take 10–14 years to reach maturity.

Play Time

From peekaboo to board games to basketball, kids like to play. So do kittens, puppies, and other young mammals. Red fox kits pounce and growl and pretend to fight each other. However, they do not really hurt each other. These "games" help the kits learn the skills they will need to hunt or fight as adults. They also help the kits develop strong muscles and coordination.

But play is not just practice for hunting. Play also helps groups of young mammals to bond and learn to trust each other. It helps the young learn their roles within the group. Play helps animals deal with stress. And it helps the brain become more creative, logical, and better at solving problems. Play isn't just for fun—it's important work!

Protective Parents

Parenthood is pretty simple if you're a mosquito or lizard. You simply lay your eggs and move on. Most amphibians, fish, reptiles, and invertebrates do not take care of their young at all. Their young act by instinct to find the resources they need and stay safe.

Young mammals, on the other hand, need lots of care in order to survive. They

EXCEPTIONS TO THE RULES

Have you ever heard the phrase, "The exception that proves the rule"? Almost every general rule in science has exceptions, or times when it doesn't apply. Mammals have their share of rule-breakers as well. For instance, as a general rule, mammals give birth to live young and do not lay eggs—except in the case of the platypus and echidna. And only female mammals make milk—except that the male Dayak fruit bat makes a small amount of milk as well. All adult mammals are warm blooded—except for the naked mole rat, which cannot keep its body temperature stable. So whenever you learn a new rule, remember—there might be an exception!

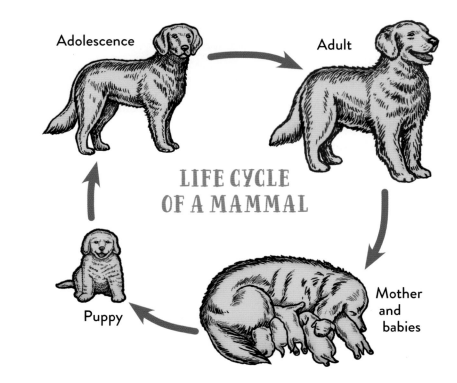

Adolescence

Adult

LIFE CYCLE OF A MAMMAL

Puppy

Mother and babies

have instincts too, but they also must learn important skills from their parents. Mammals have larger, more complicated brains than other animals do, and young mammals need time to learn to hunt for food, protect themselves, and communicate well with others of their kind. They also need their mother's milk to grow.

Some mammals are helpless when they are born—they cannot walk or even see. These animals tend to be hidden by their parents in nests. Others are born ready to move. A young wildebeest can run within hours of its birth, and a baby orca must quickly learn to swim. Even so, they need a lot of care.

In 97 percent of mammal species, fathers do not stick around to care for their young. However, some do help out. Male Eurasian beavers are very hands-on dads. They help the females to find food, guard their territory, transport and groom the kits, and huddle with them. Male meerkats, along with other females in the group, help feed and protect the young while their

Two brown bear cubs wrestle and play. *Dgwildlife/Pixabay*

mother is away hunting. Male and female African hunting dogs also work together as a pack to care for their young. When they come back from a kill, they regurgitate some food for the pups to feed on.

A Day in the Life

Imagine that you are some kind of mammal other than a human. Maybe you would like to be a cat, or a dolphin, or a tiger. What would your day be like if you were this animal?

MATERIALS

- Paper
- Pencil

1. Write a story about how you would spend your day.

   - What would you eat?
   - How would you hunt?
   - What would you be afraid of?
   - Where would you sleep?

2. Share your story with your family or classmates.

8

Mammal Chat

How do you let your friends and family know what you're thinking? You probably talk, make faces, give hugs, send text messages, and so on. Maybe you put on perfume or cologne to make yourself smell nice to others—or at least a little deodorant. That's communication as well.

They may not use social media, but other mammals communicate with each other all the time, too. They use a range of grunts, clicks, howls, smells, and touches. Each of these signals sends a message. Social animals such as wolves and primates may have as many as 30 to 40 different signals that they can send in different situations.

The two gorilla species live in Africa. *Alexas_Fotos/Pixabay*

Click, Chatter, Squeak!

Can you speak cat or squirrel? Probably not very well! Humans use words to talk to each other. We also use other sounds, like groans, screams, claps, and whistles. We understand what other people mean when they make these sounds.

Other mammals also use sounds to talk to each other. These sounds help them communicate with their babies, find mates, mark their territory, warn each other of predators, and identify themselves. It's a simple, speedy way to share information. Sound can travel around obstacles and can be heard even in the dark. It's an especially good way to talk underwater, where animals can't easily leave scent markings or visual signs. Because water is denser than air, sound travels about four times faster through water than through air.

Scientists who study mammal "talk" have found that it can be quite complex. The humpback whale's haunting song, for example, can last several hours. It travels for thousands of miles, allowing the animals to find each other even if they are far apart. Scientists disagree on the purpose of the song, but it may have to do with attracting mates or with locating objects by echolocation. At 188 decibels, a whale's song is louder than a grenade explosion or jet engine. Sounds at this level can burst human eardrums up close.

Scientists believe dolphins may speak a language similar to our own, in which they communicate using clicks and whistles. One animal will send out a pulse of sounds, and the other appears to listen before responding.

Elephants communicate by trumpeting loudly, sending low-pitched rumbles, and also by stomping their feet. Their stomps create vibrations that can be heard by other elephants up to 20 miles (32 km) away.

The howler monkey has a serious pair of lungs, which it uses to guard its territory. Its throat pouch amplifies the sound. The

SERVICE ANIMALS

Have you ever seen a dog wearing a bright red or orange vest, perhaps with a special symbol? It may be a service animal—an animal that is trained to help its owner in some special way. Service animals can signal a person with hearing loss that a phone or alarm is ringing, or help people with vision loss to find their way. They can help people walk, or pull a wheelchair. Some service animals are trained to warn their owners before they have a seizure or eat something they are allergic to, or even bring them medication or a telephone. Service animals are usually dogs, but miniature horses sometimes perform similar services for people who need assistance.

Service animals wear vests to show that they are working. **If you see a service dog, do not pet it or distract it**—it is doing a very important job! The dog knows that when its vest (and special harness) is off, it is time to relax and play.

Service dogs wear a special harness.
Found Animals Foundation/Flickr

screeches of a group of howler monkeys can be heard up to 3 miles (5 km) away. These calls can reach 90 decibels, which is loud enough to damage human hearing.

Meerkats stay in touch with each other almost constantly when they're out hunting, making soft twittering noises. They purr when they're happy and chatter when they're nervous. When a predator approaches, they give a shrill call to warn of danger.

Many other animals use sounds to warn each other, too. A dog barks or growls when it is threatened. Marmots whistle, while raccoons make a "churr churr" sound or even scream. Prairie dogs use calls to warn others in their group of approaching predators. Scientists have found that they use different calls for coyotes, humans, dogs, and hawks. These calls describe the intruder's shape, color, and size.

On the Scent

Sniff, sniff! Do you smell something? Scent is another common way that mammals send messages to each other. It is often used to mark an animal's territory. For instance, the mule deer gives off pheromones from glands inside the hind legs, outside the hind legs, between its toes, and along the lower

 TRY THIS!

Talk Like a Bat

Many bats find their food and navigate in the dark by using echolocation. They send out a series of high-pitched sounds. The sound waves bounce off objects in their surroundings—even things as tiny as a mosquito. The bat's large, sensitive ears pick up these echoes, and its brain creates a map of the objects around it. Bats are so good at this that scientists study them to make sonar systems for their ships.

How good is your echolocation? Try this activity with a friend to find out.

MATERIALS

- Blindfold
- Chair
- Ear plug

1. Put a blindfold on. Sit in a chair in the middle of the room.

2. Ask your friend to move quietly around the room. They should stop and clap their hands at various places. Try to point to the sound when you hear it. How did you do?

3. Now try the experiment again. Cup your hands behind your ears. Could you hear better?

4. Try the experiment one more time. This time, wear one ear plug. Did this make it harder to locate the sound?

edge of its eyes. These chemicals mark its territory. They also help to identify the individual, signal danger, and mark trails. Male hippos, meanwhile, spray urine and dung in a wide arc by wagging their tails in order to mark their territory. They also leave piles as signposts along the trails they travel at night.

Hyenas make a smelly paste from glands near their anus that is referred to as "hyena butter." They rub this paste onto objects and each other. It helps mark their territory and gives information about the animal that left it. Beavers also use special scents to mark their ponds. They make scent mounds by piling up mud, twigs, and

NOISE POLLUTION

It's a noisy world out there, and humans and their machines, factories, and vehicles are making it ever noisier. Unwanted or harmful levels of sound are called noise pollution. This type of pollution can affect the well-being of humans and other animals. In humans, it can raise stress levels and cause health problems ranging from lack of concentration to heart disease. For many mammals, it poses other problems. They rely on sound to find food or mates, navigate, or avoid predators. If there is too much noise around them, they cannot hear these signals. This may hurt their ability to survive.

Noise pollution is a big problem in the ocean. Ship motors, oil drills, sonar devices, and seismic testing put out loud blasts of sound or a constant hum. These sounds travel into the water itself and can especially affect whales and dolphins, which rely on echolocation for finding food, talking with each other, and finding their way around. Not only do blasts of sound make it hard for the animals to pick up these echoes, but they can also damage the animals' ears.

Mule deer give off pheromones to identify themselves, signal danger, mark danger, and tag their territory.
272447/Pixabay

leaves and spraying them with castoreum, a strong-smelling scent produced by the castor glands. These piles can be up to 5 feet (1.5 m) high!

The ring-tailed lemur uses its scent in an unusual way. When competing for mates, the males hold a "scent duel." They rub scent from glands on their wrists on to their tails. Then they flick their tails at each other so that the scent wafts through the air. They can do this for up to an hour before one gives up and runs away.

Scent can be used to keep predators away. The skunk is well known for its foul scent. It is not alone—the Tasmanian devil and striped polecat are other examples of smelly animals that use their scent to deter predators.

Scent can also be used to attract animals. Pheromones are invisible signals that let mammals know when a potential mate is in the area. The scent of a female cat, for instance, will attract males to the neighborhood. Pheromones also send other signals, such as encouraging baby rabbits to latch on to their mother's teats.

Visual Signs

Visual signals can be a tricky form of communication. Unlike sounds or smells, they only work well in the daytime, when there's enough light to see. Some of these signals are temporary. And they can't be seen from far away. Nevertheless, mammals frequently use visual signs to send messages to each other, especially animals that are active during the day and live in social groups.

One example of a visual sign is the white tail patch on a white-tailed deer. When the deer is threatened, it lifts its tail so that this white patch is visible. This behavior is called flagging. Flagging might have several purposes. First, it might distract the predator from other deer or confuse it. Or it might warn other deer that a predator is near. The deer will also stomp its feet and snort to send a warning.

The bright blue and red skin on a mandrill's face is another example of a visual signal. More-dominant males show brighter colors and higher contrast between them. These colors also brighten when the animal is excited.

Patterns on a mammal's body can send signals as well. The skunk's black-and-white patterns warn predators of its smelly spray, while a honey badger's striped mask warn of its stink bombs and ferocious bite. These signs say "Stay away!"

Body Language

When you smile, point to something, or wave to a friend, your body is sending a visual message. Sometimes you use body language on purpose and sometimes you don't even know you're doing it, but these signals are all important. Other mammals use body language in the same way. A dog wagging its tail may want to play. A stiff tail may show anxiety or a threat. A dog flattens its ears back when it is fearful or tilts them forward when it is curious.

Some primates have elaborate body language. Bonobos, for instance, loudly scratch their shoulders when they want another bonobo to groom them. A hand fling tells

Hippos make loud noises to communicate. Males also spray dung and urine to mark their territory. *Federico Torres/Pixabay*

SUPER SNIFFERS

Dogs are known as "man's best friend," and their noses can be of big help to humans. Dogs have 50 times more scent receptor cells than humans do, and 35 percent of a dog's brain is devoted to processing scent-related information. (This takes up just 5 percent of a human brain.) So it's not surprising that they're a lot better than us at following their noses.

Dogs have long been used to track missing persons by following their scent trail. Today, you might also see them in airports, train stations, and stadiums, sniffing for bombs or drugs. Dogs can be trained to sniff out electronics such as computers, cell phones, and thumb drives. Biodetection dogs can even pick up the scent of cancer, malaria, and Parkinson's Disease before a person realizes that they have the disease. Who knows what else these super sniffers may be trained to find in the future!

Make a Sound Map

Sometimes we don't notice the sounds all around us unless we listen carefully. In this activity, you will make a map of the sounds around you.

MATERIALS
- Paper
- Pen

1. Sit quietly in your chosen spot and close your eyes.

2. Draw a symbol in the center of your map to represent you. Then, when you hear a sound, mark it on your map to show which direction its coming to you from and how far away it is. Draw a little symbol to identify it—the siren of a police car, a singing bird, dripping water, etc.

3. Try this activity indoors and outdoors. Which sounds were easy to identify? Which were hard to identify? Why do you think this is?

Wolves use body language to communicate with others in their pack. *IngoMoringo/Pixabay*

other bonobos to get away. Stroking another bonobo's mouth means "give that to me"—usually referring to food. Young bonobos make faces at each other to entertain themselves. Scientists have even trained bonobos in a lab to talk to humans by pointing to symbols on a board to answer questions and communicate what they want.

Wolves use body language to show who's in charge—and who's not. For instance, the leader of a pack walks with his tail straight out, while the others' tails droop. The loser of a battle will lie down with its throat exposed to show that it is submitting to the leader. Wolves bare their teeth and perk their ears to show dominance as well.

Just a Touch

Humans like to show affection by hugging, kissing, patting each other on the back, and so on. These kinds of touch help people communicate without words. Other mammals use touch to communicate too. One common way is by grooming each other. Many mammals lick each other or use their paws to remove parasites. This helps them form bonds with other members of their group. Grooming is part of some mating rituals as well.

Newborn goat kids bump at their mother's udder to get her to let down more milk. In a similar way, puppies or kittens will knead their mother's mammary glands to release more milk.

Elephants show affection to each other by touching each other with their trunks. They lean on each other, click their tusks together, flap their ears, and intertwine their tusks. Mother elephants touch their young with their trunks and legs, and steer them by holding their tails with their trunks.

SPECIES SPOTLIGHT: Blue Whale

Can you imagine an animal as big as a house? That's the size of a blue whale! A blue whale can weigh more than 400,000 pounds (181,000 kg). Its tongue alone weighs as much as an elephant! As far as we know, the blue whale is the largest animal that has ever lived on Earth—and that includes the dinosaurs. It's also the loudest. A blue whale's call is as loud as an airplane engine. This sound can travel 1,000 miles (1,600 km).

It takes a lot of food to fuel such a huge body, but surprisingly the blue whale feeds on very small prey. It pumps ocean water through fringed plates called baleen to sift out tiny shrimplike krill. A blue whale can eat up to four tons of krill each day.

Like all mammals, baby blue whales drink milk—and a lot of it. The calf starts off weighing around 6,000 pounds (2,700 kg) and gains about 200 pounds (91 kg) per day during its first year of life. It takes a huge amount of milk to grow that fast.

Between 1900 and 1966, blue whales nearly went extinct due to overhunting. A law was passed to protect **them**, but the population has never recovered. There are only around 8,000–14,000 left in the world. And even though laws now pro-

tect them, they continue to be injured or killed by impact with ships, tangled in fishing gear, and threatened by pollution, climate change, ocean noise, and other factors.

The blue whale is the largest animal on earth. *MR1805/iStock*

Underwater Sounds

People can hear underwater, although not as well as marine animals can. Try this experiment to see how sound carries underwater. For this activity, you will need an adult's supervision and a helper.

MATERIALS

- 2 metal spoons
- Bathtub or swimming pool
- 2 plastic spoons

1. Have your friend bang the two metal spoons together. Listen carefully to the sound.

2. Now put your head underwater for a few seconds. How does the sound change?

3. Ask your friend to bang the spoons underwater. Try listening above the water, with one ear in the water, and then with your whole head underwater. How does the sound change? Where is it loudest?

4. Now repeat the experiment with the plastic spoons. Is there any difference?

9

Working with Mammals

Do you like mammals? Maybe you would like to work with them as a career. There are many different types of jobs that you can choose from. Some focus on studying and learning more about mammals and their behavior. Some work at protecting mammals and their environments. Some keep pets, livestock, and wildlife healthy.

Studying Mammals

Scientists who study animals are called zoologists. Those who specialize in mammals are called mammalogists. Marine biologists study marine mammals, along with other aquatic life. Some of these scientists study how the bodies of mammals work, some

A wild horse grazes along the coast. *James DeMers/Pixabay*

Write to an Animal Scientist

Research an animal that you are interested in. Then, with an adult's permission and help, search online for a scientist who studies that animal. You might check at a university, museum, zoo, or conservation organization. Most list their staff on their website. Write a letter or email to the scientist. Express your appreciation for their work. Ask them about their job and what they do each day. If they write back, share the letter with your class.

MATERIALS

- Internet access
- Paper
- Pen

A biologist in Illinois inspects a bat with white-nose syndrome, a disease that is deadly to bats. *US Fish and Wildlife Service Headquarters/Flickr*

study how mammals are related to each other, and some study mammal behavior. Others study how mammals fit into their environments. All of this research helps us to understand more about our world.

Conservation biologists focus on studying ecosystems and the animals in them. Wildlife biologists study wildlife populations and come up with management plans. Both types of scientists work at government agencies like the US Fish and Wildlife Service and nonprofit organizations like the Nature Conservancy to protect wild animals and their habitats.

Keeping Track

To study mammals in the wild, scientists use many different types of technology. They record mammal movement using tape recorders, cameras, and observations. Live traps can be used to catch and tag animals. Recapturing the animals later gives scientists information about their growth and population numbers.

One simple method is the camera trap. Battery-operated cameras with motion sensors are set up outdoors. When an animal's movement triggers the camera, it begins taking pictures or filming video. The photos provide information about what animals are present in an area as well as their behavior, the time of day they are active, the temperature, and so on.

Radio and satellite technology help scientists study animals as well. Land mammals such as deer and wolves can be tracked using GPS collars. These allow scientists to follow an individual animal throughout its life and keep tabs on its location. GPS batteries are too heavy for very small animals to carry. But technology is improving every year, allowing scientists to

SPECIES SPOTLIGHT: Giraffe

While the elephant is the largest land mammal, the giraffe is the tallest. An adult male can reach nearly 19 feet (6 m) in height. That means a giraffe could peer into a second-story window! A six-foot-tall man would only come up to a giraffe's belly.

Giraffes use their long necks to reach tree leaves. Their favorite leaves come from the thorny acacia tree. These trees are also home to stinging ants. That's not a problem for the giraffe, though. Its tough, 18-inch (46-cm) tongue and prehensile lips can wrap around twigs and pluck them off quickly, without injury. Giraffes chew their cud like cows do.

The giraffe's head has two bony growths called ossicones. These horns are covered with skin. Males use them to fight with each other. During mating season, they shove and push and bang their necks together.

Baby giraffes are about 6 feet (1.8 m) tall at birth. They have a long drop to the ground when they are born. Within a half hour, the baby stands and begins to nurse from its mother. After ten hours, it can run to keep up with its mother.

A giraffe's tan coat is covered with dark brown spots. The spots look different in different areas where giraffes live. They help the animal blend in with shadows under the trees.

Giraffes only need to drink every few days because of the juicy leaves they feed on. When they do take a drink, they must spread their legs wide and stretch their necks far down to reach the water. This awkward position leaves them vulnerable to predators.

Lions and crocodiles will attack giraffes, but giraffes can defend themselves well by giving the attacker a sharp kick. They can outrun a lot of predators, too, reaching speeds of up to 35 miles per hour (56 kph) for short distances.

A giraffe's horns are called ossicones. *Melanie van de Sande/Pixabay*

track more and more species. Whales can't wear collars, but they can be tracked using tags attached with suction cups. These tags use satellite technology to show where the whale goes, its depth, speed, and direction. They can even show what sounds the whale is hearing.

At the Zoo

Zoos are a fun place to see all kinds of animals. They help people learn more about different species of animals and how we can protect them. Some zoos also serve as rehabilitation centers for injured animals. If they can recover from their injuries, they are released into the wild.

Many zoos have another purpose too: they are working to save endangered species from going extinct by breeding them in captivity. Eventually their offspring may be reintroduced to the wild. These animals can start a new population of a species that has already gone extinct in the wild. Or they can boost the population of their species in the area, making it more likely that those already there can find mates and reproduce.

Releasing animals born in captivity can also increase the genetic diversity of the population. Each individual animal in a species has slightly different genes, unless

The Arabian oryx was formerly extinct in the wild. Thanks to captive breeding programs, it once again roams the Arabian Peninsula.
Leamus/iStock

it's a twin. Some individuals are better suited to their environment than others. They will be more likely to survive and pass on their genes to the next generation. But, if conditions change, different genes might become more favorable. In this way, genetic diversity helps the species survive and adapt to changing conditions.

The Arabian oryx is a captive breeding success story. These long-horned grazers live in the Middle East. In the 1970s, they

went extinct in the wild due to overhunting. But an international effort to breed them led to oryx being reintroduced to the wild in 1982, 1983, and 1990. Today there are more than 500 oryx in the wild, 300 in captivity on the Arabian Peninsula, and more than 2,000 in zoos. For now, at least, the oryx has been pulled back from the brink.

Scientists at the San Diego Zoo Safari Park are trying to save the northern white rhinoceros from extinction. The last male of the species died in 2018, and only two females are left. Neither is healthy enough to give birth, but the scientists hope to create an embryo from frozen tissue and have a southern white rhino or possibly even a horse carry the baby in its womb. They hope that within 10 years another northern white rhino might be born. The future of this species rests in their hands.

Would you like to work at a zoo? Zoos hire zookeepers to feed and take care of the animals in the zoo. They also hire veterinarians and vet assistants to help keep the animals healthy. Curators manage the zoo's collection of animals. And wildlife biologists and geneticists may work on conservation programs within the zoo. But you don't have to wait until you finish school to work at a zoo. Many zoos welcome volunteers to help with preparing food for the animals, leading tours, doing office work, and handling many other tasks.

Animal Doctors

When your pet gets sick, you can take it to a veterinarian. Veterinarians care for animals and keep them healthy. Vets not only take care of cats, dogs, and guinea pigs, but also livestock such as horses, sheep, and cattle. Wildlife veterinarians take care of sick and injured wildlife. Veterinary technicians and assistants work together with veterinarians to help take care of animals.

Wildlife rehabilitators work with injured, sick, or orphaned wild animals. Their goal is to care for them until they can be safely returned to the wild. Sometimes these animals cannot be released. If a bird cannot fly or a sea lion cannot swim, for example, it may be kept in an educational

THE FROZEN ZOO

Like a growing number of zoos and natural history museums, the San Diego Zoo is home to a surprising collection of animals—frozen ones! Since 1975, the zoo has been collecting tissues from animals to grow in the lab and then freeze at −321° F (−196° C). Some of these animals are endangered, and some are not. The approximately 1,000 species in the frozen zoo can fit into a few freezers in a single room.

These frozen materials could be used to bring extinct or endangered animals back to life, to study their genomes, or to add genetic diversity to populations. The zoo is also identifying genetic material so that meat from animals that were illegally hunted can be tested and identified.

Veterinarians take care of pets, livestock, and even wildlife.
MyFuture.com/Flickr

center where it can continue to receive care. Wildlife rehabilitators work with veterinarians to provide medical care and provide sick or injured animals with food and shelter. Special training and permits from the state are needed to become a wildlife rehabilitator. However, volunteers are often needed to help at wildlife rescue facilities. If you are interested in this career, volunteering is a great way to learn more and find out if this is a good fit for you.

On the Farm

Yet another way that people work with mammals is by farming or ranching. Animals that are raised for meat, milk, or fiber are called livestock. A farmer's job is to care for their livestock and keep them healthy and in good condition.

Wool is a soft, warm fiber that is useful for making clothing. Sheep are raised for their wool as well as for meat. Llamas and alpacas are also raised for wool in some areas. Even musk oxen can be farmed. Their heavy wool, called qiviut, is quite valuable.

Dairy farmers raise cattle or goats for their milk. The milk can be drunk directly or made into yogurt, cheese, sour cream, and other dairy products. Dairy animals must give birth each year in order to start producing milk. Farmers milk them several times a day. In some cultures and on small farms in the United States, milking is done by hand. Larger farms use milking machines. Some even use robotic milkers.

In the United States, farmers and ranchers raise cattle, pigs, sheep, and goats as well as chickens and turkeys for meat.

Many other animals, such as bison or elk, are raised for meat on a smaller scale too.

More Mammal Jobs

Did you know dogs can go to school? Obedience school, that is. Dog trainers teach dogs to follow commands and behave in ways that people want them to. Some teach

TRY THIS!

Mammals in the News

Humans aside, how have mammals been in the news recently? Perhaps there has been an outbreak of disease, or an animal escaped from a zoo. Maybe a new mammal was discovered, or a species has gone extinct. Let's find out!

MATERIALS

- Newspapers, magazines, or Internet access
- Scissors or printer

1. Scan through some recent news stories to see if you can spot any articles about mammals. If you search online, ask an adult to help you find sources.

2. Print or cut them out to share with your class.

3. What did you learn? Were the stories positive or negative? How did they help you understand animals' lives better? Has this helped you decide if working with animals is something you want to do?

basic commands such as "sit," "speak," and "heel." Others train service dogs that will help their owners cross streets safely, notify them when someone rings the doorbell, or warn them when they are about to have a seizure. Trainers may also teach police dogs to find weapons, drugs, or missing people. Some teach herding dogs to round up sheep and protect them from predators.

Pet groomers also spend their days working with dogs and cats. They help keep these animals' coats and nails trimmed and in good condition. A clean, well-groomed coat helps pets stay healthy. Pet groomers may work from home or in a pet store.

For people who like working with horses, there are many career options. Workers are needed to raise horses, train them, and groom them. Some manage horse farms or ride racehorses. Some even take care of horses' teeth or do animal massage. Farriers put horseshoes on horses.

These are just a few of the many animal-related jobs available. Would you like to start working with animals now? Perhaps you could start by pet-sitting or walking dogs. Volunteer at an animal shelter or wildlife rehabilitation center. Or just take care of pets of your own!

TRY THIS!

Write a Mammal Song

Can you think of any songs about mammals? Try writing one of your own! Maybe you'd like to write a whole song about your favorite mammal. Or maybe you'll write a song about the characteristics of mammals. Make up your own tune, or change the words to a familiar song. You may want to add musical instruments or record yourself singing your song so you can share it with others. Have fun with this!

MATERIALS
- Paper
- Pencil
- Musical instrument (optional)
- Voice recorder (optional)

Farmers and ranchers raise animals for meat, milk, and fiber. *NeiFo/Pixabay*

10

How You Can Help

It's a dangerous world out there! Half of all mammal species are decreasing in number, and more than 80 species have gone extinct in the past 50 years. Scientists estimate that one in four species is now at risk of becoming extinct. There are many reasons for this, including pollution, climate change, habitat loss, overhunting, and disease.

A Dirty World

Some human activities create pollution in the environment. Pollution can take the form of dirt, soot, chemicals, and even light, heat, and noise. Pollution can harm or kill mammals. It affects the air they breathe,

An orca leaps out of the water. *Mikhail Akkuratov/iStock*

the food they eat, and the water they drink or live in. Water pollution particularly affects marine mammals because they cannot easily escape it.

Water that falls on land and into rivers eventually ends up in the ocean. Chemicals such as DDT or PCB can run off into water from mining operations, agriculture, and offshore drilling. These are taken up by tiny animals such as zooplankton. Larger animals eat the zooplankton and are in turn eaten by still larger ones. As the chemicals move up the food chain, they become more and more concentrated. By the time they reach an apex predator, they can cause serious problems with health and reproduction.

One of these apex predators is the orca, or killer whale. Known as the "wolves of the sea," orcas hunt in packs like wolves do, herding their prey into a small area before they attack. Orcas feed mainly on marine mammals such as seals, sea lions, and even other whales, along with some fish. These prey animals can have high concentrations of pollutants in their bodies. As a result, orcas are one of the world's most contaminated marine mammals.

A Changing Climate

Another threat to mammals worldwide is our changing climate. Burning fossil fuels such as natural gas, coal, and oil puts extra carbon dioxide into the atmosphere. Burning a single gallon (3.8 L) of gasoline releases 19 pounds (8.6 kg) of this gas. The increased amount of carbon dioxide has caused the atmosphere to "thicken," and act like a greenhouse to keep more heat near the Earth. As a result, the Earth's average temperature has increased by 1.5° F (0.8° C) since 1900, and the 10 warmest years ever recorded have taken place since 1998.

This may not sound like much of an increase, but it is enough to affect the Earth's climate in serious ways. Sea levels have risen by 8 inches (20 cm) in the last century. This is because warmer water takes up more space and because of glaciers and ice sheets melting. This rise has caused more flooding in coastal areas.

Another issue is the loss of sea ice near the poles. Recent annual measurements have shown a decrease of more than 30

Burning fossil fuels puts carbon into the air, which is causing climate change. *Tama66/Pixabay*

THE GREAT PACIFIC GARBAGE PATCH

What happens to that plastic bag when you toss it out the window? It may end up swirling in a massive vortex of plastic in the Pacific Ocean. The Great Pacific Garbage Patch, which is actually two separate patches of litter, covers an area three times the size of France. It forms because of the circular way that water currents flow in the ocean. More than half of the plastic comes from North America and Asia; the rest comes from trash that is dumped by ships.

Much of the plastic here has been broken down into tiny bits called microplastics. Because plastics do not **biodegrade** for thousands of years, they simply break down into smaller and smaller bits. Mixed in are larger items such as shoes and fishing gear. The plastic does not just float on top of the water—it creates a "soup" that stretches all the way to the ocean floor. Microplastics have been found in a variety of marine mammals, but scientists don't yet know exactly how microplastics affect these animals. Some studies show that they might reduce mammal growth, foraging, and even lifespan. Perhaps you could become a researcher and help solve this micro-mystery!

Ocean debris threatens sea mammals such as seals and whales. They often get tangled in plastic fishing nets and drown. They can also swallow plastics, which makes their stomachs feel full so they stop eating. The microplastic "soup" keeps sunlight from reaching the algae and plankton below, which then produce less food for animals that feed on them. This shortage of food eventually reaches up the whole food chain.

The Atlantic and Indian Ocean have large garbage patches as well. Currently, no country has taken responsibility for cleaning up any of these garbage patches.

NOAA/Public Domain

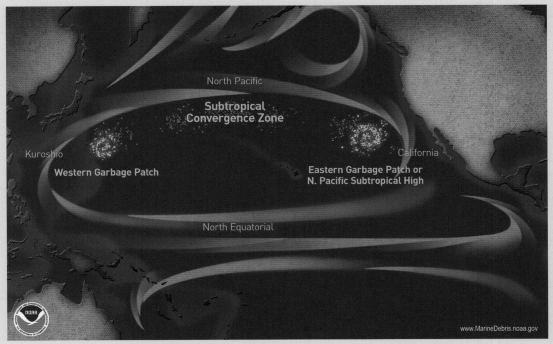

89

percent in the amount of sea-ice area during its September peaks since 1979. Sea ice helps to keep Earth's climate in balance by reflecting sunlight back into space. It also provides important hunting grounds for polar bears, seals, walruses, and other marine mammals. Without enough sea ice, they may be unable to find enough food.

The amount of precipitation is either increasing or decreasing in different parts of the world because of climate change. Some places are becoming drier, leading to more frequent wildfires, while others are getting more rain and snow. Storms are becoming more powerful and frequent. All of these changes affect wildlife habitat and animals' ability to find food and water. They also make it easier for invasive species and diseases to move into new areas and cause further devastation.

Lastly, the changing climate is making the oceans more acidic as they absorb carbon dioxide from the atmosphere. This can affect the health of the animals that live there.

Moose on the Loose

One animal that is directly threatened by climate change is the moose. These large mammals live in the northern United

 TRY THIS!

Research an Endangered Mammal

Twenty-five percent of mammal species have become endangered due to habitat loss, climate change, disease, overhunting, and other factors. With an adult's help, choose one of these mammals to research.

MATERIALS

- ♦ Internet access
- ♦ Paper or poster board
- ♦ Pen

1. Start by checking the website for the International Union for Conservation of Nature (IUCN) Red List (https://www.iucnredlist.org/) and choosing an endangered mammal.

2. Answer the following questions:

   Where does the animal live?

   Why is it threatened?

   What does the animal eat?

   What predators does the animal have?

   Are people working to protect the animal? If so, how? If not, how can you help?

3. Print or draw a picture of your mammal.

4. Put the information you have gathered into a booklet or draw a poster to share with your class, family, and friends.

States and Canada. They prefer cold climates, and when the weather is too warm, they take shelter in the shade rather than foraging for food. As a result, they lose weight, which makes them more vulnerable to disease and less able to produce healthy young.

The warmer winters have also increased the tick population in areas where moose live. Ticks feed on blood, and too much blood loss can kill the moose or cause them to rub themselves raw trying to remove these pests. In addition, the warming temperatures have caused deer to move northward into the moose's range, carrying with them a deadly parasite called brainworm.

Habitat Loss

Humans threaten mammal habitat when they cut down forests, build roads and towns, and dam or shrink rivers. This particularly affects large mammals, which need a big territory in which to forage and roam. If their territory is cut in half, they may be unable to find mates or enough food.

Tapirs have become vulnerable to extinction due to habitat loss. *johan10/iStock*

The tapir is threatened by human activity in the rain forest. The tapir looks like a cross between a pig and an elephant, but is actually related more closely to horses and rhinos. It spends a lot of its time in the water, where it uses its snorkel-like nose to breathe. The tapir feeds on fruit and leaves, using its prehensile snout to grasp them. But rain forests around the world are threatened by logging and by people

TRY THIS!

Make a Squirrel Feeder

Do you have squirrels in your neighborhood? Lure them closer with this simple squirrel feeder so you can watch their antics!

MATERIALS

- Wide-mouthed jar (a Mason jar works well)
- Wooden spoon or spatula
- Crafting wire or strong ribbon
- Whole peanuts, dried corn, hickory nuts, walnuts, or sunflower seeds (unsalted varieties)

1. With the jar standing up, hold the spoon or spatula against its side.

2. Use wire or ribbon to securely attach the spoon to the jar.

3. Turn the jar sideways. Use wire to attach it to a tree or post. Choose a spot near a window so you can watch it.

4. Fill the jar with food for the squirrels.

5. Enjoy your visitors!

burning them to build ranches and farms. As the tapir's habitat is removed, it has become vulnerable to extinction. The good news is that tapirs themselves can help to rebuild forests when they are allowed to. Their dung contains seeds that can grow in cleared areas, and they like to graze in these areas.

Human Hunters

In many places, people hunt mammals for food. Others hunt them for the pet trade or simply as trophies. Hunting can be done in a sustainable way. For instance, laws in the United States limit the number of deer that can be killed each year in order to maintain healthy population levels. Such management programs are shaped by government wildlife biologists. Hunters must have a license and report their kills to their local wildlife agency. However, many people worldwide hunt animals illegally. This is called poaching. Overhunting can cause animals to go extinct if it is not controlled.

The bison is a prime example of this. More than 50 million of these huge grazers once roamed North America. Native Americans depended on these animals for food, and they used the hides to make clothing, shelters, and canoes. When the

The bison was hunted almost to extinction in the 1800s. *WikiImages/Pixabay*

European settlers arrived, they shot bison for sport and for their hides. By 1889, fewer than 600 bison were left in the whole country. Finally, the government passed laws against hunting bison and set aside some areas to protect them. The population has grown to a half million today, although many of these are being raised for meat on ranches.

Wolves are another species with a long history of conflict with humans. Two million gray wolves once roamed the United States. However, ranchers feared them and wanted to protect their livestock, so they trapped and killed many. Along with loggers, they also destroyed much of the wolves' habitat. By the 1960s, there were very few gray wolves left in the mainland United States, with small populations in Minnesota and Michigan.

In the 1970s, the government began to protect wolves with laws against killing them. Some were resettled in Yellowstone National Park and in Idaho. This program continues to be controversial because many ranchers do not want wolves around. However, the return of the wolves has affected the ecosystem in positive ways. This experiment has taught us how important each animal in an ecosystem is to maintaining the balance of nature and showed us that wolves are a keystone species.

Rhino Rescue

The Sumatran rhinoceros is critically endangered. Once found throughout Southeast Asia, the rhino now lives only in small pockets of Indonesia, mostly on the island of Sumatra. Rhinos are herbivores and feed on fruit, twigs, and leaves. They travel at night, leaving scent trails for each other, and wallow in muddy ponds during the day.

Only a few hundred Sumatran rhinos remain in the wild. They must travel long distances to find mates. The rhinos have been hunted nearly to extinction by poachers, mostly for their horns. These were used in traditional medicines, even though studies show that they had no effect. Rhino horns were also used as dagger handles in the Middle East.

The Sumatran rhinoceros is now legally protected, and Rhino Protection Units guard their breeding areas from poachers.

An alliance formed in 2018, the Sumatran Rhino Rescue, is working to capture and move Sumatran rhinos into sanctuaries where they can be protected. Captive breeding programs in zoos are working to increase the population as well.

Deadly Disease

Disease threatens some mammal populations—especially those that are already weakened by pollution, climate change, or other factors. A deadly disease is killing large numbers of bats in the United States and Canada. Called white-nose syndrome (WNS), this disease is caused by a fungus. This white fungus grows on the bats' muzzles, ears, and wings while they are hibernating and makes them wake up more often than usual. As a result, they burn up much-needed energy during hibernation and typically starve. In some infected areas, up to 91 percent of little brown bats have died from the fungus, and researchers worry that the species may go extinct in those regions. Several other species of hibernating bats are affected as well.

Bats can catch WNS from other bats or pick up the fungus from cave walls. Humans can spread it too, if they pick up the spores on their clothing, shoes, or gear.

PYTHON PATROL

In the Florida Everglades, a marshy wilderness area, an invasive snake is devastating mammal populations. In the 1980s, people brought Burmese pythons to the state as pets. Some escaped their owners or were released into the wild when they were no longer wanted. These snakes, which can reach 23 feet (7 m) in length and weigh up to 200 pounds (91 kg), have no natural predators in Florida. In 2018, scientists noted a 99 percent decrease in fur-bearing mammals in the Everglades (mammals whose fur is valuable to trappers). Some of these species were already endangered. The snake now preys on birds and even alligators. Scientists are working at ways to eradicate the python from the Everglades, but it will be a long and difficult battle.

It is important for people who enter caves to decontaminate these items before entering another cave so they do not spread the disease.

Today, scientists are working to keep WNS from spreading to new bat populations. They are monitoring the disease and looking for ways to cure it. A recent study found that some little brown bats are resistant to the disease thanks to their genetic makeup. Bats that survived the disease had versions of two genes that might allow them to gain weight faster and hibernate more deeply.

Getting Involved

There are many ways we can all pitch in to create a healthier planet for wildlife and for humans. You can help fight climate change by using less energy from fossil fuels. Turn off lights when you are not using them. Bike or walk instead of driving when possible, and combine trips so you don't need to travel as much. Buy clothing, toys, and tools secondhand whenever you can. This keeps them out of the landfill and reduces the demand for natural resources to be spent making new ones.

You can help fight pollution by cutting down on chemicals used in your home and

SPECIES SPOTLIGHT: African Elephant

The African elephant is the largest living land mammal. It can weigh more than 6 tons (5,443 kg) and stands up to 13 feet tall. The elephant's body is covered with a tough, wrinkly hide.

The first thing you may notice about an African elephant is its giant nose, which is called a trunk. The trunk is quite useful for picking up objects, sucking up water to drink or to spray over the animal's back, and touching other elephants. The trunk is very sensitive. With nearly 40,000 muscles, it is so dexterous that it can pick a single blade of grass but is also strong enough to rip branches off a tree.

At the base of the elephant's trunk are two large ivory tusks that curve upward. These are useful for tearing bark off a tree or digging up roots for the animal to eat. Elephants are herbivores—they eat roots, leaves, grasses, fruit, and bark. They travel long distances to find food and visit several watering holes each day, where they drink and take mud baths.

Female elephants are called cows, and they give birth to one calf every two to four years. They are pregnant for about 22 months. Females travel in herds most of the times, and often help to care for each other's calves while the mother feeds.

African elephant calves may be attacked by lions, tigers, or crocodiles, but adults have few natural enemies. Their biggest threat is human hunters, who kill elephants for sport and for their ivory tusks. Today, laws protect elephants, but poachers still hunt them illegally.

The elephant is the largest living land mammal. *laurentmarx/Pixabay*

Learn About Your State Mammal

Does your state have an official state mammal? Check the list here to see.

MATERIALS

- A list of state mammals
- Internet access or books on mammals

1. Consult the list on the right to determine your state mammal. Do some research about that mammal (or mammals) in an encyclopedia or on the Internet with an adult's help to learn more about it. Why was it chosen as your state's mammal? What makes it a good symbol of your state? Indiana, Iowa, and Minnesota do not have official state mammals. If you live in one of these states, do some research about why your state doesn't have an official mammal. Perhaps you can write your legislators and suggest one!

2. Some of the states have the same mammal. Why do you think that is?

US State Mammals

United States: America Bison
Alabama: American Black Bear
Alaska: Moose, Bowhead Whale
Arizona: Ringtail
Arkansas: White-tailed Deer
California: California Grizzly Bear, Gray Whale
Colorado: Rocky Mountain Bighorn Sheep
Connecticut: Sperm Whale
Delaware: Gray Fox
Florida: Florida Panther
Georgia: White-tailed Deer, Right Whale
Hawaii: Hawaiian Monk Seal
Idaho: Appaloosa Horse
Illinois: White-tailed Deer
Indiana: None
Iowa: None
Kansas: American Bison
Kentucky: Gray Squirrel
Louisiana: American Black Bear
Maine: Moose
Maryland: Calico Cat
Massachusetts: Right Whale
Michigan: White-tailed Deer
Minnesota: None
Mississippi: White-tailed Deer, Common Bottlenose Dolphin
Missouri: Missouri Mule

Montana: Grizzly Bear
Nebraska: White-tailed Deer
Nevada: Desert Bighorn Sheep
New Hampshire: White-tailed Deer
New Jersey: Horse
New Mexico: American Black Bear
New York: Beaver
North Carolina: Gray Squirrel
North Dakota: Nokota Horse
Ohio: White-tailed Deer
Oklahoma: American Bison, White-tailed Deer, Raccoon, Mexican Free-tailed Bat
Oregon: Beaver
Pennsylvania: White-tailed Deer
Rhode Island: Harbor Seal
South Carolina: White-tailed Deer
South Dakota: Coyote
Tennessee: Raccoon
Texas: Nine-banded Armadillo, Mexican Free-tailed Bat
Utah: Rocky Mountain Elk
Vermont: Morgan Horse
Virginia: Virginia Big-Eared Bat
Washington: Olympic Marmot, Killer Whale
West Virginia: American Black Bear
Wisconsin: Badger, White-tailed Deer
Wyoming: American Bison

yard. Many of these run off into waterways or groundwater and eventually find their way to the ocean. Chemical fertilizers and pesticides are often sprayed on yards—these can be replaced by less toxic options. Try composting your yard waste and food scraps to use as natural fertilizer. Bonus: you might spot a nighttime visitor to your compost pile, like an opossum. Paints, engine oils, batteries, and electronics should be carefully disposed of, not dumped or thrown in the trash. Take them to a recycling center in your community so

the toxic chemicals they contain do not end up in the ocean.

Another way to help is by eating less meat. Large-scale animal agriculture destroys ecosystems when land is cleared, creates pollution, and uses large amounts of fresh water. Choose foods that are sustainably produced when possible. For example, cans of tuna may be labeled "dolphin-safe," meaning that the fish are caught in a way that does not kill dolphins.

Yet another way to help mammals is to join a citizen science project. No special

training is needed to help with these projects. For instance, in a bioblitz, volunteers help scientists to count all of the organisms in a specific area over a short period of time, usually 24 hours. This information can help scientists track changes in populations of plants and animals over time. You can also share information electronically with projects such as iSeeMammals.org, iNaturalist.org, or eMammal.org. Check with a nature center or park or search the Internet for more citizen science opportunities in your area.

Glossary

adaptation: A change in a species over time that allows it to better survive in its environment

anticoagulant: A substance that stops blood from clotting

apex predator: An organism that is at the very top of a food chain

arboreal: Living in trees

binomial nomenclature: The system of giving two names to each type of organism—the genus and species

biodegrade: To be broken down naturally by living organisms

blubber: The fat of a sea mammal

brachiation: Movement by swinging through the trees by the arms

carcass: The dead body of an animal

carnivore: An animal that eats meat

carrion: The decaying flesh of a dead animal

commensal: A relationship in which one organism benefits and the other is not harmed

consumer: An organism that feeds on plants or other animals for energy

countershading: A type of camouflage in which the top of an animal is darker than its underside

courtship: The behavior of animals, usually males, to attract a mate

decomposer: An organism that breaks down dead plants and animals

ecosystem: A community of living things together with the non-living parts of their environment

ectotherm: An animal whose body temperature is regulated by the outside environment

endotherm: An animal that can create heat internally

estivation: A period of dormancy during a hot, dry period

habitat: The natural home of an organism

herbivore: An animal that only eats plant materials

hibernate: To spend the winter in a dormant state

hormone: Chemicals that change an organism's physiology and behavior

instinct: A natural pattern of behavior in response to certain stimuli

invasive species: A species that is not native to a habitat, harms the ecosystem, and tends to spread

keratin: A protein that makes up hair, teeth, claws, and the like

medium: A substance or material that carries a wave

migrate: To move from one place to another according to the seasons

mutualism: A relationship in which both organisms benefit

neuron: A nerve cell

nutrient: A substance that provides nourishment to an organism

omnivore: An animal that eats both plants and animals

opposable: Able to touch other fingers on a hand or foot

overpopulate: To breed too rapidly

parasitism: A relationship in which one animal benefits and the other is harmed

pheromone: A chemical produced by an animal that affects the behavior of others of its species

placentals: Mammals that give birth to live young

poaching: Illegal hunting

pollinate: To fertilize plants by carrying pollen from one plant to another

prehensile: Able to grasp

producer: An organism that uses energy from the sun to make its own food

puberty: The period during which an animal becomes physically mature and able to reproduce

scansorial: Adapted for climbing

scavenger: An animal that feeds on dead or decaying plants or animals

symbiosis: A relationship between two organisms in which at least one benefits

taxonomy: The science of sorting animals into categories

territory: An area defended by an animal or group of animals against others

thanatosis: The defensive behavior of faking death

torpor: A state of inactivity

trophic level: The number of steps from the start of a food chain

tundra: A flat, treeless region in or near the Arctic

venomous: Able to inject toxins through a bite or sting

vertebra: One of the small bones forming the backbone in some animals

Orders of Mammals

Mammals belong to class Mammalia. They can be divided into 27 different orders. Each of these orders is subdivided into many different families.

ORDER		ORDER	
Monotremata	echidnas and platypuses	*Cingulata*	armadillos
Didelphimorphia	opossums	*Pilosa*	anteaters and sloths
Paucituberculata	shrew opossums	*Scandentia*	tree shrews
Microbiotheria	monito del monte	*Dermoptera*	colugos, flying lemurs
Notoryctemorphia	marsupial moles	*Primates*	humans, apes, monkeys, lemurs, and kin
Dasyuromorphia	carnivorous marsupials		
Peramelemorphia	bandicoots and bilbies	*Lagomorpha*	pikas, rabbits, and hares
Diprotodontia	kangaroos, koalas, wombats, possums, and kin	*Rodentia*	rodents
		Eulipotyphla	hedgehogs, shrews, moles, and kin
Tubulidentata	aardvark	*Chiroptera*	bats
Afrosoricida	golden moles and tenrecs	*Carnivora*	carnivores
Macroscelidea	elephant shrews	*Pholidota*	pangolins
Hyracoidea	hyraxes	*Perissodactyla*	odd-toed hoofed ungulates
Proboscidea	elephants	*Cetartiodactyla*	even-toed hoofed ungulates, whales, dolphins, and porpoises
Sirenia	manatees and dugongs		

Online Resources

Many organizations offer information about mammals as well as ways that students can get involved in conservation. Here are a few that you may want to start with. Check for local chapters of national organizations, nature centers, and state or national parks in your area for more possibilities.

American Society of Mammalogists
https://www.mammalsociety.org/about-mammals

Bat Conservation International
http://www.batcon.org/

eMammal
https://emammal.si.edu/

iSeeMammals
http://www.iSeeMammals.org

International Union for Conservation of Nature and Natural Resources (IUCN) Red List of Threatened Species
https://www.iucnredlist.org/

National Wildlife Federation
http://www.nwf.org

San Diego Zoo Kids
http://kids.sandiegozoo.org

World Wildlife Fund
https://www.worldwildlife.org/

A pangolin forages for food in the bush. *CarlFourie/iStockphoto*

Teacher's Guide

The activities and information in this book can be used with a wide range of ages, either in the classroom or for independent study. If you'd like to explore further, consider some of the ideas below.

- ❑ Create a word search or crossword puzzle using mammal names or words from the glossary.

- ❑ Ask students to research your state mammal and create a presentation about it. Alternatively, have each student research a different species that lives in your area and share their findings with the class.

- ❑ Research any endangered species of mammals in your area and find out how your students can get involved in protecting them.

- ❑ Make mammal conservation a focus of your Earth Day (April 22) activities.

- ❑ Have students nominate and vote on a class mammal. Research the winning species and have students draw it. Perhaps you will want to give your mammal mascot a fun name.

- ❑ Look around your neighborhood for mammal signs or tracks with your students. Or take a field trip to a local nature center or park.

- ❑ Brainstorm ways that your class can get involved with mammal conservation activities.

- ❑ Ask your students to compare and contrast the following:
  - 🐾 Marsupials
  - 🐾 Monotremes
  - 🐾 Placentals

The musk ox's heavy fur helps it survive in the Arctic. *Jonas Rönnbro/iStock*

❑ Discuss the following questions:

    🐾 What is a keystone species?

    🐾 What important roles do mammals play in the ecosystem?

    🐾 How do other mammals help humans?

    🐾 What do scientists mean when they talk about trophic levels?

    🐾 Why is it important to protect mammals?

    🐾 Which mammals make good pets, and why?

❑ Research one of these scientists further:

    🐾 Carl Linnaeus

    🐾 Charles Darwin

    🐾 Dr. Jane Goodall

    🐾 Dr. Dian Fossey

Bibliography

* *Denotes titles suitable for young readers*

Alonso, Juan Carlos. *Land Mammals of the World*. Lake Forest, CA: Walter Foster Jr., 2017.

* Daniels, Patricia. *Mammals: Ultimate Explorer Field Guide*. Washington, DC: National Geographic, 2019.

* McDougall, Len. *The Complete Tracker*. New York: Lyons & Burford, 1997.

Patent, Dorothy Hinshaw. *Saving the Tasmanian Devil*. Boston: Houghton Mifflin Harcourt, 2019.

* Walker, Sarah, and Anna Lofthouse. *Mammals (DK Eyewonder)*. New York: Dorling Kindersley Limited, 2015.

Other Resources

Many other magazine articles, scientific journal articles, and online sources were consulted during the writing of this book. These included Animal Diversity Web, National Geographic, the World Association of Zoos and Aquariums, the San Diego Zoo, Smithsonian's National Zoo & Conservation Biology Institute, and the International Union for the Conservation of Nature (IUCN), among others.

Index

Note: Page numbers in *italics* refer to photographs and illustrations.

A

aardvarks, 14
adaptations
    camouflage, 5, 26–27, 81
    countershading, 52–53
    ears, 24, *25*, *36*
    eyes, 21, *22*
    hair, 5, 25–27
    mouths, 22–24
    noses, 24
    tails, 14, 27–28, 33, 75, 76

African elephants, *x*, *94*
African wild dogs, 56
algae, 6
Animalia (kingdom), 3
anteaters, 17, *18*, 23, *50*
antelope, *8*, 56, 63
anticoagulants, 28
antlers, 56
apes, 14
apex predators, 42, 88
Arabian oryx, *82*
arboreal animals, 33
Archaebacteria (kingdom), 3
Arctic foxes, 34, *36*, 48
Arctic ground squirrels, *34*

Arctic hare, *5*
Arctic mammals, 5, 23, 34–35, 48
armadillos, 55
Artiodactyla (order), 13
Australia, 16

B

baby teeth, 42, 66
backbones, 4
bacteria, 3
badgers, 58, 75
bait balls, 56
baleen, 44
baleen whales, 12, 23

A camel closes its nostrils tightly to keep out sand. *Stephen Barnes/iStockphoto*

Barbary macaques, *65*

barnacles, 58

bats

    Dayak fruit bats, 67

    tongues of, 23

    vampire bats, *28*, 56

    white-nose syndrome (WNS), *80*,
      93–94

    wings of, 11–12

beaked dolphins, 56

bears, 34, *40*, 45–46, 63, *68*

beavers, 73–74

belly buttons, 10

binomial nomenclature, 3

bioblitzes, 96

biodegradation, 89

biologists, *80*

bison, 84, *92*

black and white stripes, *44, 53, 54,* 75

black bears, 63

blood

    of marine mammals, 24

    vampire bats and, 11–12, 28

blubber, 34

blue whales, *77*

body language, 75–76

bonobos, 75–76

bony plates, 55

brachiation, 33

brainworm, 91

breathing, 24, 36–37

breeding, 61–68, 82

Burmese pythons, 93

C

camels, 37, *106*

camera traps, 80–81

camouflage, 5, 26–27, 52–53, 81

Canada lynx, *47*

canine teeth, 42, 46

captive breeding, 82

capybaras, 10

carbon dioxide, *88*, 90

carcasses, 48

caribou, *37*, 38

carnivores, 13, 43–44

carrion, 46–47

cats, *22*, 23–24, 27, *83*

cellulose, 45

cetaceans, 12

chimpanzees, 44

Chiroptera (order), 11

Chordata (phylum), 4

citizen science projects, 96

classes, 2

climate change, 88–91

climbing mammals, 33

coccyx, 27

cochlea, 7

cold-blooded animals, 4–5

colugos, 14

commensalism, 58

communication, 71–77

consumers, 42

countershading, 52–53

courtship behaviors, 62

coyotes, 58

cud, 45

D

dairy animals, 84

Dayak fruit bats, 67

decomposers, 42–43

deer, *52*, 63, *73, 74, 75,* 91

desert mammals, 36–37

diaphragms, 7

dichotomous keys, 19

dinosaurs, 10

disease, 93–94

dogs, 56, 63, *72*, 75, 84–85

dolphins, *vii*, 12, 56, 72

dugongs, 12

E

ear bones, 7, 24, *25*

ears, 24, *25, 36*

   See also hearing

echidnas, 17, *18*, 67

echolocation, 11, 72, 74

ecosystems, xi, 42–43, 45, 52

ectotherms, 4–5

eggs, 17, 63–64

egrets, 58

elephant shrews, 14

elephants

   African elephants, *x, 94*

   characteristics of, 14

   communication of, 72

   gestation period of, 64

   humans and, 56

   noses of, 24

   territory marking and, 22–23

   touch and, 76

embryos, 63–64

endangered species

   Arabian oryx, *82*

   blue whales, *77*

   elephants, 23

   white rhinoceroses, *63*, 82

   zoos and, 82, 83

endotherms, 4–5

energy pyramid, 42, *43*

estivation, 37

Eubacteria (kingdom), 3

European mole, *33*

even-toed hoofed mammals, 13

extreme environments, 33–34

eyes, 21, *22*

eyeshine, 22

F

family classification, 2

farming, 84, *85*

fennec foxes, *36*

fetuses, 63

fingernails, 14, 23

flagging, 75

flight, 33

food chain, 42, 88

fossil fuels, *88*

foxes, *36*, 48

fruit bats, 67

Fungi (kingdom), 3

fur, 5, 26, 35

G

garter snakes, *2*

genetics, 83

genus classification, 2

gestation period, 64

gibbons, 63

gills, 24

giraffes, 24, 27, *81*

glyptodons, *10*

goats, *22*, 76

golden jackals, 58

gorillas, *70*

government agencies, 80

GPS collars, 81–82

grazing animals, 42

Great Pacific Garbage Patch, *89*

grit, 43

grizzly bears, *40*, 45–46

grooming, 27, 64–65, 76

H

habitat loss, xi, 91–92

hair, 5, 25–27

hairballs, 24

hares, 47

hearing
    adaptations and, 24–25
    ear bones, 7, *25*
    echolocation, 11
    sound waves, 13
    See also sounds and waves
heartworms, 58–59
herbivores, 13, 42, 45
herds, 56
hibernation, 34
hippopotamuses, 56, 73, *75*
honey badgers, 75
hooded seals, 62
hoofed mammals, 45, 56
hormones, 66
horses, 56, 72, *78*
howler monkeys, 72–73
humans, xi, 4
humpback whales, *12*, 43–44, 72
hunting, 92–93
hyenas, *47*, 73

I

impalas, *57*
incisors, 46
infrasonic sounds, 24–25
instincts, 61, 65, 68

invasive species, 39, 90
invertebrates, 4

J

jerboas, 27
joeys, *16*, 64

K

kangaroo rats, 37
kangaroos, 16–17, 33, 62, 64
keratin, 23, 26
keystone species, 57
kingdoms, 2–3
koalas, *16*
Kodiak bears, 45–46
krill, 43–44

L

lemurs, *22*, 74
leopards, 48
life cycle, *67*
Linnaeus, Carl, 2–4
lions, *43*, 56
livestock, 84, *85*, 92
lynxes, *47*

M

mammalogists, 79–80
mammary glands, 6
manatees, 12
mandrills, *20*, 75
marine mammals
    adaptations of, 31–32
    breathing of, 24
    migration of, 38
    noise pollution and, 74
    water pollution and, 88
marking territory, 22–23, 28, 73–74
marsupials, 14–17, 64
mating, 61–68
maturity, 66
medium, 13
meerkats, 73
megabats, 11
microplastics, 89
migration, 11, *37*, 38
milk, 6, 65–66, 77
milk teeth, 42
miniature horses, 72
molars, 42, 45, 46
molds, 3
mongooses, 57
monkeys, 14, 33, 72–73

monotremes, 17, 18, 64, 65

moose, *55*, 56, 90–91

motion, 33, 53

   See also migration

mouflons, *30*

mouths, 22–24

mule deer, 73, *74*

mushrooms, 3

musk oxen, *26*, 56, *102*

mutualism, 57–58

N

naked mole rats, 32–33, 67

naming of species, 3

narwhals, 23

neurons, 32

New World monkeys, 14

nine-banded armadillos, 55

nocturnal animals, 11, 22

noise pollution, 74

nonprofit organizations, 80

northern fur seals, 38

northern tamandua, *50*

noses, 24, 32, 75

nutrias, 39

nutrients, 6

O

odd-toed hoofed mammals, 13–14

Old World monkeys, 14

omnivores, 42, 45

opossums, 46–47, 55

opposable thumbs, 14, 24

orangutans, *66*

orcas, *86*, 88

orders, 2

overpopulation, 52

oxpeckers, *57*

P

pack hunters, 44

panda bears, 45

pangolins, 14, 43, *100*

panting, 36–37

parasites and parasitism, 58–59, 91

parents and parenthood, 67–68

Perissodactyla (order), 13–14

pets, 10, 84–85

pheromones, 62, 73–74

photography, 80–81

phylums, 2

placentals, 10

Plantae (kingdom), 3

plants, 45

platypuses, *17*, 18, 56, 67

play, 67

polar bears, 34, *35*

pollination, xi

pollution, 74, 87–88

population control, 45, 52, 92–93

porcupines, *55*

prairie dogs, *10*

precipitation, 90

predators, 42, 44

prehensile tails, 14, 33

prehistoric animals, 10

premolars, 46

pretending to be dead, 55

primates, 14, 75

producers, 42

Protista (kingdom), 3

puberty, 66

pupils, 22

pythons, 93

R

rabbits, 64–65

ranching, 84, *85*, 92

reindeer, *37*, 38

reproduction, 61–68

rhinoceroses, *27, 63*, 82, 93

robins, *2*

rodents, 10–11

rules and rule-breakers, *67*

rumen, 45

ruminants, 45

S

safety tips, xi, 7

San Diego Zoo, 82, 83

scansorial mammals, 33

scavengers, 42, 46–47

scents, 73–75

scientific names, 3

scientists

    biologists, *80*

    Linnaeus, 2–4

    mammalogists, 79–80

sea cows, 12

sea levels, 88–89

sea lions, *xii*

sea otters, 26, *32*

sea ice, 88–90

seals, *60*, 62

service animals, *72*, 84–85

short-tailed weasels, 26–27

shrews, 14

Siberian tigers, 48

single-celled organisms, 3

Sirenians, 12

skin, 27, 75

skunks, *54*, 75

sleep, 34

sloths, *6*

slow lorises, 56

smell, 24, 75

snowshoe hares, 47

social predators, 44

sounds and sound waves

    echolocation, 11, 72, 74

    hearing and, 13

    infrasonic sounds, 24–25

    noise pollution, 74

species

    classification of, 2

    endangered, 23, 77, 82, 83

    invasive, 39, 90

    keystone, 57

    naming of, 3

speed, 53

spines, 4, 18, 27, 55

spiny anteaters. *See* echidnas

spotted hyenas, *47*

squirrels, *2*, 10, 33, *34*

star-nosed moles, 32

state mammals, 95

stress, 74

stripes, 53–54, 75

sugar gliders, 33

Sumatran rhinoceroses, 27, 93

symbiosis, 57

T

tails

    overview, 27–28

    communication and, 75, 76

    prehensile, 14, 33

tapetum, 22

tapirs, *91*, 92

Tasmanian devils, *15*

taxonomies, 4

technology, 80–82, 96

teeth, 22–23, *42, 44*, 45, *46*, 66

territory marking, 22–23, 28, 73–74

thanatosis, 55

three-toed sloths, 6, 33

thumbs, 14, 24

ticks, 90–91

tigers, *48*, 56

tongues, 23–24

torpor, 34

touch, 76

tree-climbing mammals, 33

trophic levels, 42

tusks, 22–23

U

umbilical cords, 10

unicorn whales, 23

US state mammals, 95

V

vampire bats, *28*, 56

venomous mammals, 17, 56

vertebrae, 4, 27

veterinarians, *83*

Virginia opossums, 46–47

W

wallabies, *16*

walruses, 27

warm-blooded animals, 4–5

warthogs, 57

water pollution, 88–89

weaning, 6

weasels, 26–27

whales

    adaptations of, 34

    baleen whales, 12

    barnacles and, 58

    blue whales, *77*

    breathing of, 24

    humpback whales, *12*, 43–44, 72

    migration of, 38

    mouths of, 23, 43–44

    orcas, *86*, 88

whiskers, 5, 27

W

white rhinoceroses, *63*, 82

white-cheeked gibbons, 63

white-nose syndrome (WNS), *80*, 93–94

white-tailed deer, *52*, 75

white-throated wood rats, 37

wildebeests, 37–38

wildlife rehabilitators, 83–84

wolves, 44, 45, *76*, 92–93

wool, 26

Y

yeasts, 3

Yellowstone National Park, 45, 93

Z

zebras, *44*, 53

zooplankton, 88

zoos, 82–83